The Random House

Rhyming Dictionary

The Random House
Rhyming
Dictionary

Edited by Jess Stein

RANDOM HOUSE
NEW YORK

1987 Printing

Contents

Contents

Foreword

THIS DICTIONARY is more complete, more up to date, and easier to use than any other rhyming dictionary of its kind.

The user will find an abundant supply of rhyming words here for the final syllable in one list and for the last two syllables in the second list. These words have been selected with the modern user in mind. While many obsolete and rare words have been included, they have not been accumulated indiscriminately. Most importantly, a very large number of recent and common words—many not entered in much larger dictionaries—have been included.

Rhyming words have been placed under the most commonly used spelling for a particular sound. To facilitate the location of desired lists, cross references have been liberally entered.

In addition to the two lists of rhyming words, this dictionary offers the user a concise glossary of terms frequently encountered in the analysis of poetry.

Pronunciation Key

ă	act, bat	o͞o	ooze, rule
ā	able, cape	ou	out, loud
â	air, dare	p	page, stop
ä	art, calm	r	read, cry
b	back, rub	s	see, miss
ch	chief, beach	sh	shoe, push
d	do, bed	t	ten, bit
ĕ	ebb, set	th	thin, path
ē	equal, bee	t͟h	that, other
f	fit, puff	ŭ	up, love
g	give, beg	ū	use, cute
h	hit, hear	û	urge, burn
ĭ	if, big	v	voice, live
ī	ice, bite	w	west, away
j	just, edge	y	yes, young
k	kept, make	z	zeal, lazy, those
l	low, all	zh	vision, measure
m	my, him	ə	occurs only in unaccented syllables and indicates the sound of
n	now, on		a *in* alone
ng	sing, England		e *in* system
ŏ	box, hot		i *in* easily
ō	over, no		o *in* gallop
ô	order, ball		u *in* circus
oi	oil, joy		
o͝o	book, put		

One-Syllable Rhymes

-a, ah, baa, bah, blah, bra, fa, ha, ja, la, ma, pa, Ra, shah, spa; à bas, éclat, faux pas, hurrah, huzza, mama, papa, pasha, pasta, Ruy Blas; baccarat, cha cha cha, panama, Panama, Shangrila; Ali Baba, Caligula, cucaracha, tarantara; Tegucigalpa; feniculifenicula.

-ab, bab, blab, cab, crab, dab, drab, gab, grab, jab, Mab, nab, scab, slab, stab, tab; Ahab, bedab, confab, Punjab; baobab, taxicab.

-abe, Abe, babe, wabe; outgrabe; astrolabe.

-ac. See **-ack.**

-ace, ace, base, bass, brace, case, chase, dace, face, grace, Grace, lace, mace, pace, place, plaice, race, space, Thrace, trace, vase; abase, apace, birthplace, debase, deface, disgrace, displace, efface, embrace, encase, erase, footpace, grimace, horserace, misplace, outface, outpace, replace, retrace, scapegrace, staircase, ukase, uncase, unlace; about-face, boniface, carapace, commonplace, funnyface, interlace, interspace, marketplace, steeplechase.

-aced. See **-aste.**

-ach (-ăk). See **-ack.**

-ach (-ăch). See **-atch.**

-ache (-āk). See **-ake.**

-ache (-ăsh). See **-ash.**

-acht. See **-ot.**

-ack, back, black, clack, claque, crack, hack, jack, Jack, knack, lac, lack, Mac, pack,

11

plaque, quack, rack, sac, sack, sacque, shack, slack, smack, snack, stack, tack, thwack, track, whack, wrack, yak; aback, ack-ack, alack, arrack, attack, bareback, bivouac, blackjack, bootblack, cognac, drawback, Dyak, gimcrack, haystack, hogback, horse-back, humpback, hunchback, Iraq, kayak, Kodak, knickknack, macaque, Meshach, ransack, repack, rucksack, Shadrach, shellac, Slovak, ticktack, unpack, zweiback; almanac, amphibrach, applejack, bric-a-brac, Cadillac, cardiac, cul-de-sac, Frontenac, Hackensack, hackmatack, haversack, iliac, ipecac, maniac, pickaback, piggyback, Pontiac, Sarawak, stickleback, tamarack, umiak, Univac, zo-diac; ammoniac, demoniac, elegiac, sympo-siac; aphrodisiac, dipsomaniac, hypochon-driac, kleptomaniac, pyromaniac.

-acked. See **-act.**

-acks. See **-ax.**

-act, act, bract, fact, pact, tact, tract; abstract, attract, compact, contact, contract, detract, diffract, distract, enact, entr'acte, exact, extract, impact, infract, intact, protract, react, redact, refract, retract, subtract, transact; abreact, cataract, counteract, interact, over-act, re-enact, retroact, underact; matter-of-fact.

Also: **-ack** + **-ed** (as in *packed, attacked,* etc.)

-ad (-ăd), ad, add, bad, bade, brad, cad, Chad, clad, dad, fad, gad, glad, had, lad, mad, pad, plaid, sad, scad, shad, tad; Bagdad, begad, dryad, egad, footpad, forbade, gonad, monad, nomad, Pleiad, tetrad, unclad; aoudad, Dun-

ciad, hebdomad, Iliad, ironclad, Leningrad,
Petrograd, Stalingrad, Trinidad, undergrad;
olympiad.

-ad (-ŏd). See **-od**.

-ade, aid, bade, blade, braid, cade, fade, glade,
grade, jade, lade, laid, made, maid, neighed,
paid, raid, shade, spade, staid, suède, they'd,
trade, wade; abrade, afraid, alcaide, arcade,
Belgrade, blockade, brigade, brocade, cas-
cade, charade, cockade, crusade, degrade,
dissuade, evade, grenade, home-made, house-
maid, invade, limeade, mermaid, nightshade,
parade, persuade, pervade, pomade, postpaid,
prepaid, self-made, stockade, tirade, unlade,
unmade, unpaid, upbraid; accolade, Adelaide,
ambuscade, balustrade, barricade, cannon-
ade, cavalcade, centigrade, chambermaid,
colonnade, custom-made, enfilade, escalade,
escapade, esplanade, fusillade, gallopade,
gasconade, lemonade, marinade, marmalade,
masquerade, orangeade, overlade, overlaid,
palisade, plantigrade, promenade, ready-
made, renegade, retrograde, serenade, under-
paid; harlequinade, rodomontade.

   Also: **-ay** + **-ed** (as in *played*, etc.)
   Also: **-eigh** + **-ed** (as in *weighed*, etc.)
   Also: **-ey** + **-ed** (as in *preyed*, etc.)

-ade (-ăd). See **-ad**.

-ade (-ŏd). See **-od**.

-adge, badge, cadge, hadj, Madge.

-afe, chafe, safe, strafe, waif; unsafe, vouchsafe.

-aff, calf, chaff, gaff, graph, half, laugh, quaff,
staff; behalf, carafe, distaff, Falstaff, flagstaff,
giraffe, horselaugh, pikestaff, riffraff, seraph;

autograph, cenotaph, epitaph, lithograph, monograph, paragraph, phonograph, photograph, quarterstaff, shandygaff, telegraph. See also **-off.**

-affed. See **-aft.**

-aft, aft, craft, daft, draft, draught, graft, haft, kraft, laughed, raft, shaft, Taft, waft; abaft, aircraft, ingraft, seacraft, witchcraft; handicraft, overdraft.

Also: **-aff** + **-ed** (as in *staffed*, etc.)

Also: **-aph** + **-ed** (as in *autographed*, etc.)

-ag, bag, brag, crag, drag, fag, flag, gag, hag, jag, lag, nag, quag, rag, sag, scrag, shag, slag, snag, stag, swag, tag, wag; dishrag, grabbag, ragtag, sandbag, wigwag, zigzag; Brobdingnag, bullyrag, saddlebag, scalawag.

-age (-āj), age, cage, gage, gauge, page, rage, sage, stage, swage, wage; assuage, engage, enrage, greengage, outrage, presage; disengage, overage, underage.

-age (-ĭj), bridge, midge, ridge; abridge, alnage; acreage, anchorage, appanage, arbitrage, average, beverage, brokerage, cartilage, cozenage, equipage, factorage, foliage, fuselage, hemorrhage, heritage, hermitage, lineage, mucilage, overage, parentage, parsonage, pasturage, patronage, personage, pilgrimage, privilege, reportage, sacrilege, sortilege, tutelage, vicarage.

-age (-äzh), arbitrage, badinage, barrage, collage, garage, gavage, ménage, mirage, moulage; badinage, camouflage, curettage, entourage, fuselage, persiflage, reportage.

-agm. See **-am.**

-agne. See -ain.

-ague, Hague, plague, Prague, vague; fainaigue.

-ah. See -a.

-aid (-ād). See -ade.

-aid (-ĕd). See -ed.

-aif. See -afe.

-aight. See -ate.

-aign. See -ain.

-ail, ail, ale, bail, bale, Braille, dale, Dale, fail, flail, frail, Gael, Gail, gale, gaol, grail, hail, hale, jail, kale, mail, male, nail, pail, pale, quail, rail, sail, sale, scale, shale, snail, stale, swale, tail, tale, they'll, trail, vale, veil, wail, wale, whale, Yale; assail, avail, bewail, bobtail, cocktail, curtail, detail, dovetail, entail, exhale, fantail, female, hobnail, impale, inhale, prevail, regale, retail, travail, unveil, wassail, wholesale; abigail, Abigail, Bloomingdale, countervail, farthingale, ginger ale, martingale, monorail, nightingale.

-ails. See -ales.

-aim. See -ame.

-ain (-ān), Aisne, bane, blain, brain, Cain, cane, chain, crane, Dane, deign, drain, fain, fane, feign, gain, grain, Jane, lain, lane, main, Maine, mane, pain, pane, plain, plane, rain, reign, rein, sane, Seine, Shane, skein, slain, Spain, sprain, stain, strain, swain, ta'en, thane, thegn, train, twain, vain, vane, vein, wain, wane, Zane; abstain, again, airplane, amain, arcane, arraign, attain, biplane, campaign, champagne, Champlain, chicane, chilblain, chow mein, cocaine, complain, constrain, contain, demesne, detain, disdain,

distrain, dogbane, domain, Duquesne, Elaine,
enchain, entrain, ethane, explain, germane,
henbane, humane, inane, insane, Lorraine,
maintain, marchpane, membrane, methane,
moraine, murrain, obtain, ordain, pertain,
plantain, procaine, profane, ptomaine, quatrain, refrain, regain, remain, restrain, retain,
Sinn Fein, sustain, terrain, urbane; aeroplane,
appertain, ascertain, cellophane, chamber-
lain, chatelaine, counterpane, entertain, fran-
gipane, hurricane, hydroplane, monoplane,
porcelain, scatterbrain, windowpane; leger-
demain.

-ain (-ĕn). See **-en.**

-ainst, 'gainst; against.

  Also: **-ence** + **-ed** (as in *fenced*, etc.)

  Also: **-ense** + **-ed** (as in *condensed*, etc.)

-aint, ain't, faint, feint, mayn't, paint, plaint,
quaint, saint, taint; acquaint, attaint, com-
plaint, constraint, distraint, Geraint, restraint.

-aipse, traipse; jackanapes.

  Also: **-ape** + **-s** (as in *grapes*, etc.)

-air. See **-are.**

-aire. See **-are.**

-airn, bairn, cairn.

-airs. See **-ares.**

-aise (-āz). See **-aze.**

-aise (-ĕz). See **-ez.**

-ait. See **-ate.**

-aith, eighth, faith, Faith, wraith.

-aize. See **-aze.**

-ak. See **-ack.**

-ake, ache, bake, Blake, brake, break, cake,
crake, drake, fake, flake, hake, Jake, lake,

make, quake, rake, sake, shake, slake, snake,
spake, stake, steak, strake, take, wake;
awake, backache, bespake, betake, cornflake,
daybreak, earache, earthquake, forsake,
heartbreak, keepsake, mandrake, mistake,
namesake, opaque, outbreak, partake, retake,
snowflake, sweepstake, toothache; bellyache,
johnnycake, overtake, patty-cake, rattle-
snake, stomach ache, undertake.

-al, Al, Hal, pal, sal, shall; banal, cabal, canal,
corral, locale, morale, Natal, timbale; fal-
deral, musicale; Guadalcanal.

-ald, bald, scald; piebald, so-called; Archibald.
  Also: **-all** + **-ed** (as in *stalled*, etc.)
  Also: **-aul** + **-ed** (as in *hauled*, etc.)
  Also: **-awl** + **-ed** (as in *crawled*, etc.)

-ale (-āl). See **-ail.**

-ale (-ăl). See **-al.**

-ales, Wales; entrails, marseilles, Marseilles.
  Also: **-ail** + **-s** (as in *fails*, etc.)
  Also: **-ale** + **-s** (as in *scales*, etc.)

-alf. See **-aff.**

-alk, auk, balk, calk, chalk, gawk, hawk,
squawk, stalk, talk, walk; catwalk, Mohawk;
tomahawk; Manitowoc; Oconomowoc.

-all (-ăl). See **-al.**

-all (-ôl). See **-awl.**

-alled. See **-ald.**

-alm, alm, balm, calm, Guam, palm, psalm,
qualm; becalm, embalm, madame, salaam.

-alp, alp, Alp, palp, scalp.

-alt (-ôlt), fault, halt, malt, salt, smalt, vault;
asphalt, assault, basalt, cobalt, default, exalt;
somersault.

-alt (-ălt), alt, shalt.

-alts. See **-altz.**

-altz, waltz.

Also: **-alt** + **-s** (as in *salts*, etc.)

Also: **-ault** + **-s** (as in *faults*, etc.)

-alve, calve, halve, have, salve, Slav, suave;
Zouave.

-am, am, cam, Cham, clam, cram, dam, damn,
drachm, dram, gram, ham, jam, jamb, lam,
lamb, ma'am, Pam, pram, ram, Sam, scram,
sham, slam, swam, tram, wham, yam; Assam,
flimflam, madame, Siam; Abraham, aero-
gram, Alabam, Amsterdam, Birmingham,
anagram, cablegram, cryptogram, diagram,
diaphragm, dithyramb, epigram, hexagram,
marjoram, monogram, Rotterdam, Surinam,
telegram; ad nauseam, radiogram; parallelo-
gram.

-amb. See **-am.**

-ame, aim, blame, came, claim, dame, fame,
flame, frame, game, lame, maim, Mame,
name, same, shame, tame; acclaim, aflame,
became, beldame, declaim, defame, disclaim,
exclaim, inflame, misname, nickname, pro-
claim, reclaim, surname; overcame.

-amp (-ămp), amp, camp, champ, clamp, cramp,
damp, guimpe, lamp, ramp, scamp, stamp,
tamp, tramp, vamp; decamp, encamp, fire-
damp, revamp; afterdamp.

-amp (-ŏmp). See **-omp.**

-an (-ăn), an, Ann, Anne, ban, bran, can, clan,
Dan, fan, Fran, Jan, Klan, man, Nan, pan,
Pan, plan, ran, scan, span, tan, than, van;
afghan, Afghan, began, corban, dishpan,

divan, fantan, foreran, he-man, Iran, japan,
Japan, Koran, Milan, pavan, pecan, rattan,
sedan, trepan, unman; Alcoran, artisan,
astrakhan, Astrakhan, caravan, catalan,
courtesan, Hindustan, overran, Pakistan,
partisan, spick-and-span. Turkestan; Afghan-
istan, catamaran, orang-utan.

-an (-ŏn). See **-on**.

-ance, chance, dance, France, glance, hanse,
lance, manse, pants, prance, stance, trance;
advance, askance, bechance, enhance, en-
trance, expanse, finance, mischance, per-
chance, romance; circumstance.

   Also: **-ant** + **-s** (as in *grants*, etc.)

-anch, blanch, Blanche, branch, ganch, ranch,
stanch; carte blanche; avalanche.

-anct, sacrosanct.

   Also: **-ank** + **-ed** (as in *spanked*, etc.)

-and (-ănd), and, band, bland, brand, gland,
grand, hand, land, rand, sand, stand, strand,
Strand; backhand, command, demand, dis-
band, expand, forehand, Greenland, remand,
unhand, withstand; ampersand, contraband,
countermand, fairyland, fatherland, four-in-
hand, hinterland, Holy Land, overland,
reprimand, Rio Grande, Samarcand, sara-
band, underhand, understand, wonderland;
misunderstand, multiplicand, Witwatersrand.

   Also: **-an** + **-ed** (as in *banned*, etc.)

-and (-ŏnd). See **-ond**.

-ane. See **-ain**.

-ang, bang, bhang, clang, fang, gang, gangue,
hang, pang, rang, sang, slang, sprang, stang,
tang, twang, whang, yang; harangue, me-

ringue, mustang, Penang, shebang; boomerang; orangoutang.

-ange, change, grange, mange, range, strange; arrange, derange, estrange, exchange; disarrange, interchange, rearrange.

-angue. See -ang.

-ank, bank, blank, clank, crank, dank, drank, flank, franc, frank, Frank, hank, Hank, lank, plank, prank, rank, sank, shank, shrank, spank, stank, swank, tank, thank, yank, Yank; embank, outflank, outrank, pointblank, snowbank; mountebank.

-anked. See -anct.

-anned. See -and.

-anse. See -ance.

-ant (-ănt), ant, aunt, can't, cant, chant, grant, Grant, Kant, pant, plant, rant, scant, shan't, slant; aslant, decant, descant, displant, enchant, extant, gallant, implant, Levant, recant, supplant, transplant; adamant, commandant, disenchant, gallivant; hierophant.

-ant (-ŏnt). See -aunt.

-ants. See -ance.

-ap, cap, chap, clap, flap, gap, hap, Jap, lap, map, nap, pap, rap, sap, scrap, slap, snap, strap, tap, trap, wrap, yap; claptrap, dunce cap, entrap, enwrap, foolscap, kidnap, madcap, mayhap, mishap, nightcap, unwrap; afterclap, handicap, overlap, rattletrap, thunderclap.

-ape, ape, cape, chape, crepe, drape, grape, jape, nape, rape, scrape, shape, tape; agape, escape, landscape, seascape, shipshape, undrape.

-apes. See **-aipse.**

-aph. See **-aff.**

-aphed. See **-aft.**

-apped. See **-apt.**

-aps. See **-apse.**

-apse, apse, craps, lapse, schnapps; collapse, elapse, perhaps, relapse.

    Also: **-ap** + **-s** (as in *claps*, etc.)

-apt, apt, rapt, wrapt; adapt.

    Also: **-ap** + **-ed** (as in *clapped*, etc.)

-aque. See **-ack.**

-ar (-är), Aar, are, bar, car, char, czar, far, jar, Loire, mar, par, parr, Saar, scar, spar, star, tar, tsar; afar, agar, ajar, armoire, bazaar, bizarre, catarrh, cigar, couloir, Dakar, debar, disbar, felspar, guitar, horse-car, hussar, lascar, Navarre, pourboire; Alcazar, au revoir, avatar, caviar, cinnabar, registrar, reservoir, samovar, seminar, Zanzibar; agar-agar.

-ar (-ôr). See **-or.**

-arb, barb, garb; rhubarb.

-arce. See **-arse.**

-arch, arch, larch, march, March, parch, starch; outmarch; countermarch.

-arch. See **-ark.**

-ard (-ärd), bard, card, chard, guard, hard, lard, nard, pard, sard, shard, yard; Bernard, bombard, canard, discard, foulard, Gerard, lifeguard, petard, placard, regard, retard; Abelard, avant-garde, bodyguard, boulevard, disregard, Hildegarde, interlard, leotard; camelopard.

    Also: **-ar** + **-ed** (as in *starred*, etc.)

-ard (-ôrd). See **-ord.**

-are, air, Ayr, bare, bear, blare, care, chair,
Claire, dare, e'er, ere, fair, fare, flair, flare,
gare, glair, glare, hair, hare, heir, herr, lair,
mare, mayor, ne'er, pair, pare, pear, Pierre,
prayer, rare, scare, share, snare, spare,
square, stair, stare, swear, tare, tear, their,
there, they're, ware, wear, where, yare;
affair, armchair, aware, beware, coheir,
compare, corsair, declare, despair, eclair,
elsewhere, ensnare, fanfare, forbear, forswear,
Gruyère, horsehair, howe'er, impair, mohair,
Mynheer, nightmare, outstare, prepare, re-
pair, unfair, welfare, whate'er, whene'er,
where'er; anywhere, Camembert, croix de
guerre, debonair, Delaware, doctrinaire,
earthenware, étagère, everywhere, Frigidaire,
laissez faire, maidenhair, mal de mer,
millionaire, nom de guerre, outerwear, porte-
cochere, solitaire, thoroughfare, unaware,
underwear; vin ordinaire.

-ares, theirs; downstairs, upstairs; unawares.
Also: **-air** + **-s** (as in *stairs*, etc.)
Also: **-are** + **-s** (as in *dares*, etc.)
Also: **-ear** + **-s** (as in *swears*, etc.)
Also: **-eir** + **-s** (as in *heirs*, etc.)

-arf, corf, dwarf, wharf; endomorph, meso-
morph, perimorph.

-arge, barge, charge, large, marge, Marge,
sarge; discharge, enlarge, surcharge; over-
charge, supercharge, undercharge.

-ark, arc, ark, bark, barque, cark, Clark, dark,
hark, lark, mark, Mark, marque, park, sark,
shark, snark, spark, stark; aardvark, Bis-

marck, debark, embark, landmark, remark, tanbark; disembark, hierarch, matriarch, oligarch, patriarch.

-arl, carl, Carl, gnarl, marl, snarl.

-arm (-ärm), arm, barm, charm, farm, harm, marm; alarm, disarm, forearm, gendarme, schoolmarm, unarm.

-arm (-ôrm). See **-orm.**

-arn (-ärn), barn, darn, Marne, tarn, yarn.

-arn (-ôrn). See **-orn.**

-arp (-ärp), carp, harp, scarp, sharp; escarp; counterscarp, pericarp.

-arp (-ôrp). See **-orp.**

-arred. See **-ard.**

-arse, farce, parse, sparse.

-arsh, harsh, marsh.

-art (-ärt), art, Bart, cart, chart, dart, hart, heart, mart, part, smart, start, tart; apart, depart, dispart, impart, sweetheart, upstart; counterpart.

-art (-ôrt). See **-ort.**

-arth. See **-orth.**

-arts. See **-artz.**

-artz, courts, shorts, quartz.

  Also: **-art** + **-s** (as in *warts*, etc.)

  Also: **-ort** + **-s** (as in *sorts*, etc.)

-arve, carve, starve.

-as (-ŏz), Boz, vase, was; La Paz.

-as (-ä). See **-a.**

-as (-ăs). See **-ass.**

-ase (-ās). See **-ace.**

-ase (-āz). See **-aze.**

-ased. See **-aste.**

-ash (-ăsh), ash, bash, brash, cache, cash,

clash, crash, dash, flash, gash, gnash, hash,
lash, mash, Nash, pash, plash, rash, sash, slash,
smash, splash, thrash, trash; abash, calash,
mishmash, moustache, panache, Wabash;
balderdash, calabash, sabretache, succotash.

-ash (-ŏsh), bosh, gosh, gauche, josh, posh,
quash, slosh, squash, swash, wash; apache,
awash, galosh, goulash; mackintosh.

-ask, ask, bask, Basque, cask, casque, flask,
mask, masque, Pasch, task; unmask.

-asm, chasm, plasm, spasm; orgasm, phantasm,
sarcasm; cataplasm, pleonasm, protoplasm;
enthusiasm, iconoclasm.

-asp, asp, clasp, gasp, grasp, hasp, rasp;
enclasp, unclasp.

-ass, ass, bass, brass, class, crass, gas, glass,
grass, lass, mass, pass; alas, amass, crevasse,
cuirasse, harass, impasse, morass, paillasse,
repass, surpass; demitasse, hippocras, looking
glass, sassafras, underpass.

-assed. See -ast.

-ast, bast, blast, cast, caste, fast, hast, last,
mast, past, vast; aghast, avast, bombast,
contrast, forecast, outcast, peltast, repast,
steadfast; flabbergast, overcast; ecclesiast,
enthusiast, iconoclast.

Also: -ass + -ed (as in *passed*, etc.)

-aste, baste, chaste, haste, paste, taste, waist,
waste; distaste, foretaste, unchaste; after-
taste.

Also: -ace + -ed (as in *placed*, etc.)

Also: -ase + -ed (as in *chased*, etc.)

-at (-ăt), at, bat, brat, cat, chat, drat, fat, flat,
gat, ghat, gnat, hat, mat, Matt, Nat, pat,

Pat, plat, rat, sat, slat, spat, sprat, tat, that,
vat; combat, cravat, fiat, muskrat, polecat,
whereat, wombat; acrobat, Ararat, autocrat,
Automat, democrat, diplomat, habitat, he-
mostat, Kattegat, photostat, plutocrat, ther-
mostat, tit for tat; aristocrat.

-at (-ä). See **-a.**

-at (-ŏt). See **-ot.**

-atch (-ăch), batch, catch, hatch, latch, match,
patch, scratch, snatch, thatch; attach, detach,
dispatch, mismatch, unlatch; bandersnatch.

-atch (-ŏch). See **-otch.**

-ate, ait, ate, bait, bate, crate, date, eight, fate,
fête, frate, freight, gait, gate, grate, great,
hate, Kate, late, mate, Nate, pate, plait,
plate, prate, rate, sate, skate, slate, spate,
state, straight, strait, trait, wait, weight;
abate, aerate, agnate, alate, await, baccate,
berate, bookplate, bromate, casemate, cas-
trate, caudate, cerate, checkmate, chelate,
chlorate, chromate, cirrate, citrate, classmate,
cognate, collate, comate, connate, cordate,
costate, create, cremate, crenate, crispate,
cristate, curate, curvate, debate, deflate,
delate, dentate, dictate, dilate, donate, elate,
equate, estate, falcate, filtrate, flyweight,
formate, frontate, frustrate, furcate, gem-
mate, globate, gradate, guttate, gyrate,
hamate, hastate, helpmate, hydrate, inflate,
ingrate, inmate, innate, instate, irate, jugate,
khanate, lactate, larvate, legate, lichgate,
ligate, lightweight, lobate, locate, lunate,
lustrate, magnate, mandate, messmate, mi-
grate, misdate, mismate, misstate, mutate,·

narrate, negate, nervate, nictate, nitrate, notate, nutate, oblate, orate, ornate, ovate, palate, palmate, palpate, peltate, pennate, phonate, phosphate, picrate, pinnate, placate, playmate, prelate, primate, private, probate, prolate, prorate, prostate, prostrate, pulsate, punctate, quadrate, quinate, rebate, relate, restate, rotate, rugate, sedate, septate, serrate, shipmate, sigmate, spicate, stagnate, stalemate, stannate, stellate, striate, sublate, sulcate, sulfate, tannate, tartrate, template, ternate, testate, titrate, tractate, translate, truncate, vacate, vibrate, Vulgate, xanthate, zonate; abdicate, ablactate, abnegate, abrogate, accurate, acetate, actuate, addlepate, adequate, adulate, adumbrate, advocate, aggravate, aggregate, agitate, allocate, altercate, alternate, ambulate, amputate, animate, annotate, annulate, antedate, antiquate, apostate, appellate, approbate, arbitrate, arrogate, aspirate, aureate, aviate, bifurcate, Billingsgate, brachiate, bracteate, branchiate, cachinnate, calculate, calibrate, caliphate, cancellate, candidate, captivate, carbonate, castigate, catenate, celibate, cellulate, chloridate, ciliate, circulate, clypeate, cochleate, cogitate, colligate, collimate, collocate, comminate, compensate, complicate, concentrate, confiscate, conformate, conglobate, congregate, conjugate, consecrate, constipate, consulate, consummate, contemplate, copulate, cornuate, coronate, corporate, correlate, corrugate, corticate, coruscate, crenellate, crenulate, crepitate, cucullate, culminate, cultivate, cumulate, cuneate, cuspidate, cyanate, decimate, declinate, decollate, decorate, decussate, dedicate, defalcate, defecate, dehydrate, delegate, delicate, demarcate, demonstrate, denigrate, denudate, depilate, deprecate, depredate, derogate, desecrate, desiccate, designate, desolate, desperate, detonate, devastate, deviate, digitate, diplomate, dislocate, disparate, dissipate, distillate, divagate, doctorate, dominate, duplicate, ebriate, echinate, edentate, educate, elevate, elongate, emanate, emigrate, emulate, enervate, eructate, estimate, estivate, excavate, exculpate, execrate, expiate, explanate, explicate, expurgate, extirpate, extricate, fabricate, fascinate, featherweight, fecundate, federate, fenestrate, fibrillate, fistulate, flagellate, floriate, fluctuate, fluorate, foliate, formicate, formulate, fornicate, fortunate, fructuate, fulgurate, fulminate, fumigate, geminate, generate, germinate, glaciate, gladiate, glomerate, graduate, granulate, gravitate, heavyweight, hebetate, hesitate, hibernate, hyphenate, ideate, illustrate, imbricate, imitate, immigrate, immolate, implicate, imprecate, impregnate, improvisate, incarnate, inchoate, incrassate, incubate, inculcate, inculpate, incurvate, indicate, indurate, infiltrate, innervate, innovate, inornate, insensate, insolate, inspissate, instigate, insufflate, insulate, integrate, interstate, intestate, intimate, intonate, intricate, inundate, irrigate, irritate, isolate, iterate, jubilate, khedivate, labiate, lacerate, lamellate, laminate, lancinate, lapidate, laureate, legislate, levirate levitate, liberate, ligulate, lineate, liquidate, literate, litigate, loricate, lubricate, lucubrate, macerate, machinate, maculate, magistrate, majorate, manducate, manganate, marginate, margravate, marquisate, masticate, maturate, mediate, medicate, meditate, menstruate, methylate, micturate, militate, mitigate, moderate, modulate, molybdate, motivate, muriate, mutilate, nauseate, navigate, nictitate, niobate, nominate, nucleate, obfuscate, objurgate, obligate, obovate, obstinate, obviate, oculate, oleate, omoplate, opiate, orchestrate, ordinate, oscillate, oscitate, osculate, overrate, overstate, overweight, ovulate, paginate, palliate, palpitate, paperweight, papillate, passionate, pastorate, patellate, pectinate, peculate, pejorate, pendulate, penetrate, percolate, perforate, permeate, perorate, perpetrate, personate, phosphorate, pileate, pollinate, populate, postulate, potentate, predicate, principate, priorate, procreate, profligate, promulgate, propagate, propinquate, proximate, prussiate, pullulate, pulmonate, pulverate, pulvinate, punctuate, punctulate, pustulate, radiate, radicate, reclinate, recreate, rectorate, recurvate, regulate, reinstate, relegate, remigrate, remonstrate, renovate, replicate, reprobate, resonate, roseate, rostellate, rubricate, ruminate, rusticate, sagittate, salivate, sanitate, satiate, saturate, scintillate, scutellate, segmentate, segregate, selenate, separate, septenate, sequestrate, seriate, serrulate, shogunate, sibilate, silicate, simulate, sinuate, situate, spatulate, speculate, spiculate, spiflicate, spoliate, staminate, stearate, stellulate, stimulate, stipulate, strangulate, stylobate, subjugate, sublimate, subulate, suffocate, sulfurate, sultanate, supinate, supplicate, suppurate, surrogate, syncopate, syndicate, tabulate, tellurate, temperate, tête-à-tête, titanate, titillate, titivate, tolerate, toluate, trabeate, tracheate, transmigrate, tridentate, trijugate, trilobate, triplicate, trisulcate, triturate, tubulate, tunicate, turbinate, ulcerate, ultimate, ululate, umbellate, uncinate, undulate, underrate, understate, underweight, ungulate, urinate, urticate, ustulate, vaccinate, vacillate, vaginate, valerate, validate, vanillate, variate, vegetate, venerate, ventilate, vertebrate, vesicate, vindicate, violate, viscerate, vitiate, welterweight; abbreviate, abominate, accelerate, accentuate, accommodate, accumulate, acidulate, acuminate, adjudicate, adulterate, affectionate, affiliate, agglomerate, agglutinate, aldermanate, alienate, alleviate, amalgamate, annihilate, annunciate, anticipate, apiculate, apostolate, appreciate, appropinquate, appropriate, approximate, areolate, articulate, asphyxiate, assassinate, asseverate, assimilate, associate, attenuate, auriculate, authenticate, calumniate, capitulate, cardinalate, centuplicate, certificate, chalybeate, circumvallate, coagulate, coelenterate, collaborate, collegiate, commemorate, commensurate, commiserate, communicate, compassionate, concatenate, conciliate, confabulate, confed-

erate, conglomerate, conglutinate, congratu-
late, considerate, consolidate, contaminate,
conterminate, continuate, cooperate, coor-
dinate, corroborate, corymbiate, curvicau-
date, curvicostate, debilitate, decapitate,
decemvirate, degenerate, deglutinate, delib-
erate, delineate, denominate, denticulate,
denunciate, depopulate, depreciate, deraci-
nate, desiderate, determinate, debranchiate,
dictatorate, dilapidate, directorate, discon-
solate, discriminate, dispassionate, dissemi-
nate, dissimulate, dissociate, divaricate,
domesticate, duumvirate, ebracteate, effec-
tuate, effeminate, ejaculate, elaborate, elec-
torate, electroplate, eliminate, elucidate,
emaciate, emancipate, emasculate, enucleate,
enumerate, enunciate, episcopate, equilibrate,
equivocate, eradiate, eradicate, etiolate,
evacuate, evaginate, evaluate, evaporate,
eventuate, eviscerate, exacerbate, exaggerate,
exanimate, exasperate, excogitate, excoriate,
excruciate, exfoliate, exhilarate, exonerate,
expatiate, expatriate, expectorate, expostu-
late, expropriate, exsanguinate, extenuate,
exterminate, extortionate, extravagate, exu-
berate, facilitate, felicitate, foraminate, ge-
latinate, geniculate, gesticulate, habilitate,
habituate, hallucinate, horripilate, humiliate,
hydrogenate, hypothecate, illiterate, illumi-
nate, immaculate, immediate, immoderate,
imperforate, impersonate, importunate, im-
postumate, impropriate, inaccurate, inade-
quate, inanimate, inaugurate, incarcerate,
incinerate, incorporate, incriminate, indeli-

cate, indoctrinate, inebriate, infatuate, infu-
riate, ingeminate, ingratiate, ingurgitate,
initiate, innominate, inoculate, inordinate,
insatiate, inseminate, inseparate, insinuate,
inspectorate, intemperate, intercalate, inter-
minate, interpolate, interrogate, intimidate,
intoxicate, invaginate, invalidate, inverte-
brate, investigate, inveterate, inviduate,
invigorate, inviolate, irradiate, irradicate,
itinerate, lanceolate, legitimate, licentiate,
lineolate, lixiviate, luxuriate, machicolate,
mandibulate, manipulate, marsupiate, matri-
archate, matriculate, meliorate, miscalculate,
multidentate, multilobate, multiplicate, ne-
cessitate, negotiate, nidificate, novitiate,
nudirostrate, obliterate, officiate, operate,
operculate, orbiculate, orientate, originate,
oxygenate, pacificate, palatinate, paniculate,
participate, particulate, patriarchate, pedicu-
late, penultimate, peregrinate, permanganate,
perpetuate, petiolate, pomegranate, pontifi-
cate, postgraduate, precipitate, precogitate,
preconsulate, predestinate, predominate, prej-
udicate, premeditate, prenominate, prevari-
cate, procrastinate, prognosticate, proliferate,
propitiate, proportionate, protectorate, pro-
tuberate, quadruplicate, quintuplicate, reani-
mate, recalcitrate, reciprocate, recriminate,
recuperate, redecorate, reduplicate, refriger-
ate, regenerate, regurgitate, reiterate, rejuve-
nate, remunerate, repatriate, repopulate,
repudiate, resuscitate, retaliate, reticulate,
reverberate, salicylate, somnambulate, so-
phisticate, subordinate, substantiate, syllabi-

cate, tergiversate, testiculate, testudinate, trabeculate, transliterate, triangulate, tricorporate, trifoliate, triumvirate, variegate, vermiculate, vesiculate, vestibulate, vicariate, vituperate, vociferate; ameliorate, baccalaureate, canaliculate, circumambulate, circumnavigate, circumstantiate, consubstantiate, deoxygenate, deteriorate, differentiate, discombobulate, disproportionate, domiciliate, excommunicate, imbecilitate, incapacitate, intermediate, latifoliate, misappropriate, predeterminate, proletariate, quadrifoliate, quadrigeminate, quinquefoliate, ratiocinate, recapitulate, rehabilitate, reinvigorate, secretariate, superannuate, supererogate, transubstantiate, trifoliolate, undergraduate, unifoliate.

-ath (-ăth), bath, Bath, Gath, hath, lath, math, path, rath, snath, wrath; bypath; aftermath, allopath, psychopath; homeopath, osteopath.

-ath (-ôth). See **-oth.**

-athe, bathe, lathe, scathe, swathe; unswathe.

-auce. See **-oss.**

-aud, bawd, broad, Claude, fraud, gaud, laud, Maud; abroad, applaud, belaud, defraud, maraud.

Also: **-aw** + **-ed** (as in *clawed*, etc.)

-augh. See **-aff.**

-aught. See **-ought** or **-aft.**

-aul. See **-awl.**

-auled. See **-ald.**

-ault. See **-alt.**

-aunch, craunch, haunch, launch, paunch, staunch.

-aunt, aunt, daunt, flaunt, gaunt, haunt, jaunt, taunt, vaunt, want; avaunt, romaunt.

-aunts. See **-once.**

-ause, cause, clause, gauze, hawse, pause, yaws; applause, because.

Also: **-aw** + **-s** (as in *claws*, etc.)

-aust. See **-ost.**

-aut. See **-ought.**

-ave (-āv). See **-alve.**

-ave (-āv), brave, cave, crave, Dave, gave, glaive, grave, knave, lave, nave, pave, rave, save, shave, slave, stave, suave, they've, waive, wave; behave, concave, conclave, deprave, enclave, engrave, enslave, exclave, forgave, margrave, misgave, octave; architrave.

-aw, awe, caw, chaw, claw, craw, daw, draw, faugh, flaw, gnaw, haw, jaw, law, maw, paw, pshaw, raw, saw, Shaw, squaw, straw, taw, thaw, yaw; catspaw, coleslaw, cushaw, foresaw, gewgaw, guffaw, heehaw, jackdaw, jigsaw, macaw, papaw, seesaw, southpaw, Warsaw, withdraw; Arkansas, overawe, usquebaugh.

-awd. See **-aud.**

-awed. See **-aud.**

-awk. See **-alk.**

-awl, all, awl, ball, bawl, brawl, call, crawl, drawl, fall, gall, Gaul, hall, haul, mall, maul, pall, Paul, pawl, Saul, scrawl, shawl, small, sprawl, squall, stall, tall, thrall, trawl, wall, yawl; appall, baseball, befall, Bengal, catcall, enthrall, football, footfall, forestall, install, rainfall, recall, snowfall, windfall; alcohol, basketball, caterwaul, overhaul, pentothal, waterfall, wherewithal.

-awled. See **-ald.**

-awn, awn, bawn, brawn, dawn, drawn, faun, fawn, gone, lawn, pawn, prawn, sawn, Sean, spawn, yawn; indrawn, withdrawn.

-aws. See **-ause.**

-ax, ax, flax, lax, Max, pax, sax, tax, wax; addax, Ajax, anthrax, climax, relax, syntax; battleax, Halifax, Kallikaks, parallax; Adirondacks, anticlimax.

Also: **-ack** + **-s** (as in *sacks*, etc.)

-ay, a, aye, bay, bey, brae, bray, clay, day, dray, ey, fay, Fay, fey, flay, fray, gay, gray, greige, grey, hay, jay Kay, lay, Mae, may, May, nay, née, neigh, pay, play, pray, prey, ray, Ray, say, shay, slay, sleigh, spay, spray, stay, stray, sway, they, trait, tray, trey, way, weigh, whey; abbé, affray, agley, allay, array, assay, astray, away, belay, beret, betray, bewray, Bombay, bomb bay, bouquet, café, Calais, Cathay, causeway, chambray, convey, Coué, coupé, Courbet, croquet, curé, decay, defray, delay, dengue, dismay, display, distrait, doomsday, dragée, endplay, essay, filet, fillet, foray, Fouquet, foyer, Friday, gainsay, gangway, hearsay, heyday, horseplay, inlay, inveigh, Malay, Manet, melee, midday, mislay, moiré, Monday, Monet, moray, nosegay, obey, okay, ole!, passé, per se, pince-nez, portray, prepay, purée, purvey, relay, repay, risqué, Roget, roué, sachet, sashay, soirée, soufflé, subway, Sunday, survey, throughway, Thursday, today, tokay, touché, toupée,

Tuesday, waylay, Wednesday; appliqué,
cabaret, canapé, castaway, Chevrolet, con-
sommé, deMusset, disarray, disobey, dis-
tingué, émigré, exposé, faraway, holiday,
Mandalay, matinee, Milky Way, Monterey,
Monterrey, negligée, Nez Percé, popinjay,
protégé(e), résumé, roundelay, runaway,
Saint-Tropez, Salomé, Santa Fe, Saturday,
s'il vous plait, sobriquet, stowaway, virelay,
yesterday; Appian Way, cabriolet, café au
lait, caloo-calay, communiqué, habitué,
papier-maché, sotto voce, Tono-Bunday;
Edna St. Vincent Millay.

-ayed. See -ade.

-ays. See -aze.

-aze, baize, blaze, braise, braze, chaise, craze,
daze, faze, gaze, glaze, graze, haze, maize,
maze, phase, phrase, praise, raise, raze;
ablaze, amaze, appraise, dispraise; chryso-
prase, Marseillaise, mayonnaise, nowadays,
paraphrase, polonaise.
　　Also: -ay + -s (as in *days*, etc.)
　　Also: -ey + -s (as in *preys*, etc.)
　　Also: -eigh + -s (as in *weighs*, etc.)

-azz, as, has, jazz, razz; topaz, whereas;
Alcatraz, razzmatazz.

-e. See -ee.

-ea. See -ee.

-eace. See -ease.

-each, beach, beech, bleach, breach, breech,
each, leech, peach, preach, reach, screech,
speech, teach; beseech, impeach; over-
reach.

-ead (-ēd). See -eed.

-ead (-ĕd). See **-ed.**

-eaf (-ĕf). See **-ef.**

-eaf (-ēf). See **-ief.**

-eague, Grieg, klieg, league; colleague, enleague, fatigue, intrigue.

-eak (-ēk), beak, bleak, cheek, chic, clique, creak, creek, eke, freak, Greek, leak, leek, meek, peak, peek, pique, reek, seek, sheik, shriek, Sikh, sleek, sneak, speak, squeak, streak, teak, tweak, weak, week, wreak; antique, bespeak, bezique, cacique, critique, Monique, mystique, oblique, physique, relique, unique; Chesapeake, Frederique, Martinique, Mozambique, Pathétique.

-eak (-āk). See **-ake.**

-eal, ceil, creel, deal, eel, feel, heal, heel, he'll, keel, Kiel, kneel, leal, meal, Neal, Neil, peal, peel, real, reel, seal, she'll, spiel, squeal, steal, teal, veal, weal, we'll, wheel, zeal; anele, anneal, appeal, Bastille, cartwheel, Castile, chenille, conceal, congeal, Émile, genteel, ideal, Lucille, misdeal, mobile, Mobile, pastille, repeal, reveal, unreal; cochineal, commonweal, deshabille, glockenspiel, mercantile; automobile.

-eald. See **-ield.**

-ealed. See **-ield.**

-ealm. See **-elm.**

-ealth, health, stealth, wealth; commonwealth.

-eam, beam, bream, cream, deem, dream, fleam, gleam, ream, scheme, scream, seam, seem, steam, stream, team, teem, theme; abeam, beseem, blaspheme, centime, daydream, esteem, extreme, ice cream, moonbeam, redeem, regime, supreme, trireme; academe; ancien régime.

-ean, bean, been, clean, dean, Dean, e'en, Gene, glean, green, Jean, keen, lean, lien, mean, mien, peen, preen, quean, queen, scene, screen, seen, sheen, spleen, teen, wean, ween, yean; baleen, beguine, benzine, between, caffein, canteen, careen, chlorine, Christine, codeine, colleen, convene, cuisine, demean, demesne, eighteen, Eileen, Eugene, fifteen, foreseen, fourteen, ich dien, Kathleen, machine, marine, nineteen, obscene, Pauline, poteen, praline, protein, quinine, ravine, routine, sardine, serene, shagreen, sixteen, subvene, thirteen, tontine, tureen, unclean; Aberdeen, Abilene, Argentine, atabrine, atropine, barkentine, Benzedrine, bombazine, brigantine, contravene, crêpe de chine, damascene, evergreen, fellahin, Florentine, gabardine, gasoline, Geraldine, Ghibelline, guillotine, intervene, Josephine, kerosene, libertine, magazine, mezzanine, Nazarene, nectarine, nicotine, overseen, Paris green, quarantine, serpentine, seventeen, submarine, tambourine, tangerine, unforeseen, Vaseline, velveteen, wolverine; acetylene, aquamarine, elephantine, incarnadine, ultramarine.

-eaned. See **-iend.**

-eant. See **-ent.**

-eap. See **-eep.**

-ear. See **-eer.**

-earch. See **-urch.**

-eard (-ĩrd), beard, tiered, weird; afeard.

Also: **-ear** + **-ed** (as in *reared*, etc.)

Also: **-ere** + **-ed** (as in *interfered*, etc.)

Also: **-eer** + **-ed** (as in *veered*, etc.)

-eard (-ûrd). See **-urd.**

-eared. See **-eard.**

-earl. See **-url.**

-earn. See **-urn.**

-ears. See **-ares.**

-earse. See **-erse.**

-eart. See **-art.**

-earth. See **-irth.**

-eas. See **-ease.**

-ease (-ēs), cease, crease, fleece, geese, grease, Greece, lease, Nice, niece, peace, piece; caprice, decease, decrease, increase, Maurice, obese, police, release, surcease, valise; ambergris, frontispiece, mantelpiece, masterpiece, Singalese.

-ease (-ēz), bise, breeze, cheese, ease, freeze, frieze, grease, he's, lees, pease, please, seize, she's, skis, sneeze, squeeze, tease, these, wheeze; appease, Bernice, Burmese, cerise, chemise, Chinese, disease, displease, Louise, Maltese, Thales, trapeze; ABC's, Achilles, Androcles, antifreeze, Antilles, Balinese, Cantonese, Heloise, Hercules, Japanese, Javanese, journalese, obsequies, overseas, Pekingese, Portuguese, Siamese, Viennese; anopheles, antipodes, antitheses, Hippocrates, hypotheses, parentheses, soliloquies; aborigines.

Also: **-ea** + **-s** (as in *teas*, etc.)

Also: **-ee** + **-s** (as in *bees, frees*, etc.)

-eased. See **-east.**

-east, beast, east, feast, least, priest, yeast;
artiste.

Also: **-ease** + **-ed** (as in *released*, etc.)

-eat (-ēt), beat, beet, bleat, cheat, Crete, eat,
feat, feet, fleet, greet, heat, meat, meet, mete,
neat, peat, Pete, pleat, seat, sheet, skeet,
sleet, street, suite, sweet, teat, treat, wheat;
accrete, aesthete, afreet, athlete, compete,
complete, conceit, concrete, deadbeat, deceit,
defeat, delete, deplete, discreet, discrete,
effete, elite, entreat, petite, receipt, replete,
retreat, secrete; bittersweet, Easy Street,
incomplete, indiscreet, obsolete, overeat,
parrakeet.

-eat (-āt). See **-ate.**

-eat (-ĕt). See **-et.**

-eath (-ĕth), Beth, breath, death, saith, Seth;
Macbeth; Elizabeth, shibboleth.

-eath (-ēth), heath, Keith, 'neath, sheath, teeth,
wreath; beneath; underneath.

-eathe, breathe, seethe, sheathe, teethe, wreath;
bequeath, enwreathe.

-eau. See **-ow.**

-eave, breve, cleave, eave, eve, Eve, grieve,
heave, leave, lieve, peeve, reave, reeve, sleeve,
Steve, thieve, weave, we've; achieve, aggrieve,
believe, bereave, conceive, deceive, khedive,
naïve, perceive, qui vive, receive, relieve,
reprieve, retrieve; disbelieve, interleave,
make-believe.

-eb, bleb, deb, ebb, neb, reb, web; sub-deb.

-eck, beck, check, cheque, Czech, deck, fleck,
heck, neck, peck, reck, speck, tech, trek,

wreck; bedeck, henpeck, Quebec; Tehuan-
tepec.

-ecked. See **-ect.**

-ecks. See **-ex.**

-ect, sect; abject, affect, bisect, collect, connect,
correct, defect, deflect, deject, detect, direct,
dissect, effect, eject, elect, erect, expect,
infect, inject, inspect, neglect, object, pan-
dect, perfect, prefect, project, prospect, pro-
tect, reflect, reject, respect, select, subject,
suspect; architect, circumspect, dialect, dis-
connect, disrespect, incorrect, intellect, inter-
ject, intersect, introspect, misdirect, recollect,
retrospect, vivisect.

Also: **-eck** + **-ed** (as in *wrecked*, etc.)

-ed, bed, bled, bread, bred, dead, dread, Ed,
fed, fled, Fred, head, Jed, lead, led, Ned,
pled, read, red, said, shed, shred, sled, sped,
spread, stead, ted, Ted, thread, tread, wed,
zed; abed, ahead, behead, biped, coed, hogs-
head, inbred, instead, misled, outspread,
unread, unsaid; aforesaid, gingerbread, log-
gerhead, quadruped, thoroughbred, underfed,
watershed.

-ede. See **-eed.**

-edge, dredge, edge, fledge, hedge, kedge, ledge,
pledge, sedge, sledge, wedge; allege, unedge.

-ee, be, Bea, bee, Cree, fee, flea, flee, free, gee,
glee, he, key, knee, lea, lee, me, pea, plea,
quay, sea, see, she, ski, spree, tea, thee, three,
tree, we, wee, ye; acme, acne, agree, bohea,
debris, decree, degree, Dundee, ennui, fore-
see, goatee, grandee, grantee, lessee, levee,
Marie, marquee, marquis, Parsee, rupee,

settee, spondee, trochee, trustee; ABC,
abscissae, absentee, adobe, addressee, agony,
alumnae, anomie, anomaly, amputee, apogee,
assignee, Athene, baloney, botany, bour-
geoisie, bumblebee, calorie, calumny, canopy,
cap-a-pie, Cherokee, chickadee, chimpanzee,
C.O.D., company, coterie, DDT, debauchee,
destiny, devotee, disagree, ebony, felony,
filagree, fleur-de-lis, fricassee, gluttony, guar-
antee, harmony, irony, jamboree, licensee,
Lombardy, Maccabee, maître d', manatee,
Niobe, nominee, Normandy, pedigree, peri-
gee, Pharisee, Picardy, potpourri, Ptolemy,
recipe, referee, refugee, repartee, reveille,
Sadducee, sesame, symphony, syzygy, tyr-
anny, vis-a-vis; abalone, anemone, apos-
trophe, Antigone, Ariadne, calliope, catastro-
phe, Euphrosyne, facsimile, Gethsemane
hyperbole, macaroni, Melpomene, Penelope,
proclivity, synonymy; aborigine, Deuteron-
omy.

-eece. See **-ease.**

-eech. See **-each.**

-eed, bead, Bede, bleed, breed, cede, creed,
deed, feed, freed, greed, heed, keyed, knead,
lead, mead, Mede, meed, need, plead, read,
reed, seed, screed, speed, steed, Swede, tweed,
weed; concede, decreed, exceed, impede,
indeed, misdeed, mislead, precede, proceed,
recede, secede, stampede, succeed; aniseed,
antecede, centipede, Ganymede, intercede,
millipede, overfeed, supersede; velocipede;
Niebelungenlied.

Also: **-ee** + **-ed** (as in *agreed*, etc.)

-eef. See **-ief.**

-eek. See **-eak.**

-eel. See **-eal.**

-eeled. See **-ield.**

-eem. See **-eam.**

-een. See **-ean.**

-eened. See **-iend.**

-eep, cheap, cheep, creep, deep, heap, jeep, keep, leap, neap, peep, reap, seep, sheep, sleep, steep, sweep, veep, weep; asleep, beweep; oversleep.

-eer, beer, bier, blear, cheer, clear, dear, deer, drear, ear, fear, fleer, gear, hear, here, jeer, Lear, leer, mere, near, peer, pier, queer, rear, sear, seer, sere, shear, sheer, smear, sneer, spear, sphere, steer, tear, tier, veer, weir, year; adhere, Aegir, amir, ampere, appear, arrear, austere, brassière, career, cashier, cashmere, cohere, compeer, emir, endear, frontier, inhere, reindeer, revere, severe, sincere, Tangier, veneer; atmosphere, auctioneer, bandoleer, bombardier, brigadier, buccaneer, cannoneer, cavalier, chandelier, chanticleer, chiffonier, commandeer, disappear, domineer, engineer, financier, frontier, gazeteer, gondolier, grenadier, hemisphere, insincere, interfere, jardiniere, mountaineer, muleteer, musketeer, mutineer, overhear, overseer, pamphleteer, persevere, pioneer, privateer, profiteer, sonneteer, souvenir, volunteer; charioteer.

-eered. See **-eard.**

-ees. See **-ease.**

-eese. See **-ease.**

-eet. See **-eat.**

-eethe. See **-eathe.**

-eeze. See **-ease.**

-ef, chef, clef, deaf, Jeff; Khrushchev.

-eft, cleft, deft, eft, heft, left, reft, theft, weft; bereft.

-eg, beg, dreg, egg, keg, leg, Meg, peg, Peg, skeg, yegg; nutmeg, pegleg; philibeg, Winnipeg.

-ege (-ĕzh), barège, cortege, manège.

-ege (-īj). See **-age.**

-egm. See **-em.**

-eigh. See **-ay.**

-eighed. See **-ade.**

-eighs. See **-aze.**

-eight (-āt). See **-ate.**

-eight (-īt). See **-ite.**

-eign. See **-ain.**

-eil (-āl). See **-ail.**

-eil (-ēl). See **-eal.**

-ein (-ān). See **-ain.**

-ein (-īn). See **-ine.**

-eint. See **-aint.**

-eir. See **-are.**

-eird. See **-eard.**

-eirs. See **-ares.**

-eive. See **-eave.**

-eize. See **-ease.**

-eke. See **-eak.**

-el, bell, belle, Belle, cell, dell, dwell, ell, fell, hell, jell, knell, Nell, quell, sell, shell, smell, spell, swell, tell, well, yell; appel, befell, compel, Cornell, dispel, Estelle, excel, expel, foretell, gazelle, hotel, impel, lapel, Moselle,

pastel, pell-mell, rebel, repel; asphodel,
Astrophel, bagatelle, calomel, caravel, caro-
mel, citadel, clientele, decibel, hydromel,
infidel, Jezebel, muscatel, parallel, personnel,
philomel, pimpernel, sentinel, undersell,
villanelle; mademoiselle.

-elch, belch, squelch.

-eld, eld, geld, held, weld; beheld, unquelled,
upheld, withheld.

Also: **-ell** + **-ed** (as in *spelled*, etc.)

-elf, delf, elf, Guelph, pelf, self, shelf; herself,
himself, itself, myself, ourself, thyself, your-
self.

-elk, elk, whelk.

-ell. See **-el.**

-elle. See **-el.**

-elled. See **-eld.**

-elm, elm, helm, realm, whelm; overwhelm.

-elp, help, kelp, whelp, yelp; self-help.

-elt, belt, Celt, dealt, dwelt, felt, Kelt, knelt,
melt, pelt, smelt, spelt, svelte, veldt, welt.

-elve, delve, helve, shelve, twelve.

-em, em, femme, gem, hem, phlegm, Shem,
stem, them; adquem, ad rem, ahem, begem,
condemn, contemn, pro tem; apothegm,
Bethlehem, diadem, requiem, stratagem,
theorem; ad hominem.

-eme. See **-eam.**

-emn. See **-em.**

-empt, dreamt, kempt, tempt; attempt, con-
tempt, exempt, pre-empt, unkempt.

-en, Ben, den, fen, glen, Gwen, hen, ken, men,
pen, ten, then, wen, when, wren, yen, Zen;
again, amen, Cheyenne; allergen, citizen,

hydrogen, nitrogen, oxygen, Saracen, specimen; comedienne, equestrienne, Parisienne, tragedienne.

-ence, cense, dense, fence, hence, pence, sense, tense, thence, whence; commence, condense, defense, dispense, expense, Hortense, immense, incense, intense, offense, pretense, suspense; abstinence, accidence, affluence, ambience, audience, confidence, consequence, continence, difference, diffidence, diligence, eloquence, eminence, evidence, excellence, frankincense, immanence, imminence, impotence, impudence, indigence, indolence, inference, influence, innocence, negligence, opulence, penitence, preference, providence, recompense, redolence, reference, residence, reticence, reverence, sapience, truculence, turbulence, vehemence, violence, virulence; beneficence, benevolence, circumference, grandiloquence, inconsequence, intelligence, intransigence, magnificence, munificence, obedience, omnipotence, pre-eminence, subservience.

Also: **-ent** + **-s** (as in *tents*, etc.)

-enced. See **-ainst**

-ench, bench, blench, clench, drench, flench, French, quench, stench, tench, trench, wench, wrench; intrench, retrench.

-end, bend, blend, end, fend, friend, lend, mend, rend, send, spend, tend, trend, vend, wend; amend, append, ascend, attend, befriend, commend, contend, defend, depend, descend, distend, emend, expend, extend, forefend, impend, intend, misspend, offend, pitchblende, portend, pretend, stipend, suspend, transcend, unbend; apprehend, comprehend, condescend, dividend, minuend, recommend, reprehend, subtrahend; overextend, superintend.

Also: **-en** + **-ed** (as in *penned*, etc.)

-ene. See **-ean.**

-enge, avenge, revenge; Stonehenge.

-ength, length, strength; full-length.

-enned. See **-end.**

-ens. See **-ense.**

-ense (-ĕns). See **-ence.**

-ense (-ĕnz), cleanse, gens, lens.

Also: **-en** + **-s** (as in *pens*, etc.)

Also: **-end** + **-s** (as in *bends*, etc.)

-ensed. See **-ainst.**

-ent, bent, blent, cent, dent, gent, Ghent, Kent, leant, lent, Lent, meant, pent, rent, scent, sent, spent, tent, Trent, vent, went; absent, accent, anent, ascent, assent, augment, cement, comment, consent, content, descent, detent, dissent, event, extent, ferment, foment, frequent, indent, intent, invent, lament, misspent, portent, present, prevent, relent, repent, resent, torment, unbent, unspent; abstinent, accident, aliment, argument, armament, banishment, battlement, betterment, blandishment, chastisement, competent, complement, compliment, condiment, confident, consequent, continent, detriment, different, diffident, diligent, dissident, document, element, eloquent, eminent, evident, excellent, exigent, filament, firmament, fraudulent, government, immanent, imminent, implement, impotent, impudent, incident, increment, indigent, innocent, insolent, instrument, languishment, liniment, malcontent, management, measurement, merriment, monument, negligent, nourishment, nutriment, occident, opulent, orient, ornament, overspent, parliament, penitent, permanent, pertinent, precedent, president, prevalent, prisonment, provident, punishment, ravishment, redolent, regiment, represent, resident, reticent, reverent, rudiment, sacrament, sentiment, settlement, subsequent, succulent, supplement, tenement, testament, underwent, vehement, violent, virulent, wonderment; accomplishment, acknowledgment, advertisement, astonishment, belligerent, benevolent, development, disarmament, embarrassment, embodiment, enlightenment, environment, establishment, experiment, impenitent, impertinent, imprisonment, improvident, intelligent, irreverent, magnificent, magniloquent, presentiment, subservient, temperament; accompaniment.

-ep, hep, nep, pep, prep, rep, repp, step, steppe, yep; Dieppe, footstep; demirep; Amenhotep.

-ept, drept, kept, sept, slept, stepped, swept, wept; accept, adept, except, inept, y-clept; intercept, overslept.

-er, blur, bur, burr, cur, err, fir, fur, her, myrrh, per, purr, shirr, sir, slur, spur, stir, were, whir; astir, aver, Ben Hur, bestir, Big Sur, chasseur, chauffeur, coiffeur, concur, confer, defer, demur, deter, hauteur, incur, infer, inter, occur, prefer, recur, refer, transfer;

amateur, arbiter, barrister, calendar, chron-
icler, chorister, colander, comforter, connois-
seur, cylinder, de rigueur, disinter, dowager,
gossamer, harbinger, Jennifer, Jupiter, lav-
ender, Lucifer, mariner, massacre, messenger,
minister, officer, passenger, prisoner, register,
scimitar, sepulcher, traveler, voyageur;
administer, astrologer, astronomer, barom-
eter, Excalibur, idolater, thermometer.

-erb, blurb, curb, herb, kerb, Serb, verb; acerb,
adverb, disturb, perturb, suburb, superb.

-erce. See -erse.

-erced. See -urst.

-erch. See -urch.

-erd. See -urd.

-ere (-ār). See -are.

-ere (-ēr). See -eer.

-ered. See -eard.

-erf. See -urf.

-erg, berg, burgh; iceberg.

-erge, dirge, merge, purge, scourge, serge,
splurge, spurge, surge, urge, verge; absterge,
converge, deterge, diverge, emerge, immerge,
submerge; demiurge, dramaturge, thauma-
turge.

-erm. See -irm.

-ern. See -urn.

-err. See -er.

-erred. See -urd.

-erse, curse, Erse, hearse, herse, nurse, purse,
terse, verse, worse; accurse, adverse, amerce,
asperse, averse, coerce, commerce, converse,
disburse, disperse, diverse, imburse, immerse,
inverse, obverse, perverse, rehearse, reverse,

traverse, transverse; intersperse, reimburse, universe.

-ersed. See **-urst.**

-ert, Bert, blurt, Burt, curt, dirt, flirt, Gert, girt, hurt, Kurt, pert, shirt, skirt, spurt, squirt, wert, wort; advert, Albert, alert, assert, avert, concert, convert, covert, desert, dessert, divert, evert, exert, expert, filbert, Herbert, inert, insert, invert, overt, pervert, revert, subvert, unhurt; controvert, discontcert, extrovert, introvert; animadvert.

-erth. See **-irth.**

-erve, curve, Irv, nerve, serve, swerve, verve; conserve, deserve, incurve, innerve, observe, outcurve, preserve, reserve, unnerve.

-es. See **-ess.**

-esce. See **-ess.**

-ese. See **-ease.**

-esh, crêche, flesh, fresh, mesh, thresh; afresh, enmesh, immesh, refresh.

-esk. See **-esque.**

-esque, desk; burlesque, grotesque, Moresque; alhambresque, arabesque, humoresque, picaresque, picturesque, Romanesque, statuesque.

-ess, Bess, bless, cess, chess, cress, dress, guess, jess, Jess, less, mess, press, stress, Tess, tress, yes; abscess, access, actress, address, aggress, assess, caress, compress, confess, countess, depress, digress, distress, duress, egress, empress, excess, express, finesse, impress, ingress, largesse, Loch Ness, mattress, noblesse, obsess, oneness, oppress, possess, princess, profess, progress, recess, redress, repress, success, suppress, transgress, undress, unless; acquiesce, baroness, coalesce, comfortless, convalesce, dispossess, effervesce, Inverness, obsolesce, opalesce, overdress, poetess, politesse, prophetess, repossess, shepherdess, sorceress, votaress, wilderness; nevertheless, proprietress.

Also: many words with the suffix **-ness** (as in *smallness*, etc.) and **-less** (as in *homeless*, etc.)

-esse. See **-ess.**

-essed. See **-est.**

-est, best, blest, breast, Brest, chest, crest, geste, guest, jest, lest, nest, pest, quest, rest, test, vest, west, wrest, zest; abreast, arrest, attest, behest, bequest, Celeste, congest, contest, detest, digest, divest, incest, infest, inquest, invest, Key West, molest, protest, request, suggest, unblest, unrest; acid test, alkahest, Almagest, anapest, Budapest, Everest, manifest; disinterest.

Also: **-ess + -ed** (as in *pressed*, etc.)

Also: many superlative forms ending in **-est** (as in *happiest*, etc.)

-et, bet, debt, fret, get, jet, let, Lett, met, net, pet, Rhett, set, stet, sweat, threat, tret, vet, wet, whet, yet; abet, aigrette, Annette, barrette, beget, beset, brochette, brunette, cadet, Claudette, Colette, coquette, corvette, curvet, duet, egret, forget, gazette, grisette, Jeannette, octet, offset, omelet, quartet, quintet, regret, rosette, roulette, septet, sestet, sextet, soubrette, Tibet, upset, vignette; alphabet, amulet, anisette, banneret, baronet, bassinet, bayonet, cabinet, calumet, castanet, cigarette, clarinet, coronet, epaulet, epithet, etiquette, Juliet, marmoset, martinet, mignonette, minaret, minuet, parapet, pirouette, quadruplet, quintuplet, rivulet, serviette, silhouette, suffragette, tourniquet, violet, winterset; marionette.

-etch, etch, fetch, ketch, retch, sketch, stretch, vetch, wretch; outstretch.

-ete. See **-eat.**

-eth. See **-eath.**

-ette. See **-et.**

-euce. See **-use.**

-eud. See **-ude.**

-eur. See **-er.**

-euth. See **-ooth.**

-eve. See **-eave.**

-ew, blew, blue, boo, brew, chew, clue, coo, coup, crew, cue, dew, do, drew, due, ewe, few, flew, flu, flue, glue, gnu, goo, grew, hew, hue, Hugh, Jew, knew, Lew, lieu, loo, Lou, mew, moo, mu, new, nu, pew, phew, queue, rue, screw, shoe, shrew, skew, slew, slough, sou, spew, stew, strew, sue, Sue, thew, threw, through, to, too, true, two, view, who, woo, yew, you, zoo; accrue, adieu, ado, ague, Ainu, Andrew, Anjou, anew, askew, bamboo, bedew, cachou, canoe, cashew, cuckoo, curfew, curlew, debut, emu, endue, ensue, eschew, Hindu, imbue, issue, juju, menu, mildew, Peru, pooh-pooh, pursue, purview, ragout, renew, review, shampoo, subdue, taboo, tattoo, tissue, undo, venue, voodoo, withdrew, yahoo, Zulu; avenue, barbecue, billet-doux, catechu, cockatoo,

curlicue, interview, kangaroo, misconstrue,
parvenu, rendezvous, residue, retinue, rev-
enue, toodle-oo, Timbuktu; Kalamazoo,
merci beaucoup.

-ewd. See **-ude.**

-ews. See **-ooze** and **-use.**

-ewt. See **-ute.**

-ex, ex, flex, hex, lex, rex, Rex, sex, specs,
vex; annex, apex, codex, complex, convex,
index, perplex, reflex; circumflex.
Also: **-eck** + **-s** (as in *pecks*, etc.)

-exed. See **-ext.**

-ext, next, text; pretext.
Also: **-ex** + **-ed** (as in *vexed*, etc.)

-ey (-ā). See **-ay.**

-ey (-ē). See **-ee.**

-eyed. See **-ade.**

-eys. See **-aze.**

-ez, fez, says; Juarez, malaise, Suez; Marseillaise.

-i (ē). See **-ee.**

-i (ī). See **-y.**

-ib, bib, crib, dib, drib, fib, glib, jib, nib, rib,
sib, squib; ad-lib, Carib.

-ibe, bribe, gibe, jibe, scribe, tribe; ascribe
describe, imbibe, inscribe, prescribe, pro-
scribe, subscribe, transcribe; circumscribe,
diatribe, superscribe.

-ic. See **-ick.**

-ice, bice, Brice, dice, ice, gneiss, lice, mice,
nice, price, rice, slice, spice, splice, thrice,
trice, twice, vice, vise; advice, allspice, concise, device, entice, precise, suffice; edelweiss,
overnice, paradise, sacrifice.

-iced. See **-ist.**

-ich. See **-itch.**

-ick, brick, chic, chick, click, crick, dick, Dick,
flick, hick, kick, lick, mick, nick, Nick, pick,
prick, quick, rick, sic, sick, slick, snick, stick,
thick, tick, trick, Vic, wick; beatnik, caustic,
heartsick, lovesick, sputnik, toothpick, triptych, yardstick; acoustic, arsenic, artistic,
bailiwick, Benedick, bishopric, Bolshevik,
candlestick, candlewick, catholic, chivalric,
choleric, double-quick, fiddlestick, heretic,
limerick, lunatic, maverick, Menshevik,
pogostick, politic, rhetoric, turmeric; arch-
bishopric, arithmetic, cataleptic, impolitic.

-icked. See **-ict.**

-icks. See **-ix.**

-ict, Pict, strict; addict, afflict, conflict, con-
strict, convict, depict, evict, inflict, predict,
restrict; benedict, Benedict, contradict, dere-
lict, interdict.

Also: **-ick** + **-ed** (as in *picked*, etc.)

-id, id, bid, chid, Cid, did, grid, hid, kid, lid,
mid, quid, rid, skid, slid, squid; amid, Enid,
eyelid, forbid, gravid, Madrid, outbid, outdid,
rabid, undid; arachnid, insipid, invalid, katy-
did, overbid, pyramid, underbid; caryatid.

-ide, bide, bride, chide, Clyde, glide, guide,
hide, pied, pride, ride, side, slide, snide,
stride, tide, wide; abide, aside, astride, back-
side, backslide, beside, bedside, bestride,
betide, broadside, bromide, carbide, cock-
eyed, collide, confide, cowhide, cross-eyed,
decide, deride, divide, elide, green-eyed,
hillside, horsehide, inside, misguide, noon-

tide, one-eyed, outside, oxide, pop-eyed,
preside, provide, reside, seaside, subside, sul-
fide, wall-eyed, wayside, Yuletide, worldwide;
almond-eyed, alongside, Barmecide, bona-
fide, Christmastide, coincide, dioxide, Easter-
tide, eventide, fratricide, genocide, homocide,
iodide, matricide, monoxide, mountainside,
open-eyed, override, parricide, peroxide,
regicide, subdivide, suicide, Whitsuntide;
aborticide, formaldehyde, infanticide, insec-
ticide, tyrannicide, uxoricide.

    Also: **-ie** + **-d** (as in *lied*, etc.)

    Also: **-igh** + **-ed** (as in *sighed*, etc.)

    Also **-y** + **-ed** (as in *cried*, etc.)

-ides, ides; besides.

    Also: **-ide** + **-s** (as in *tides, hides*, etc.)

-idge. See **-age.**

-idst, bidst, chidst, didst, hidst, midst, ridst;
amidst, forbidst.

-ie (-ē). See **-ee.**

-ie (-ī). See **-y.**

-iece. See **-ease.**

-ied. See **-ide.**

-ief, beef, brief, chief, fief, feoff, grief, leaf, lief,
reef, sheaf, thief; belief, fig leaf, relief; bas
relief, disbelief, handkerchief, interleaf, neckerchief, Tenerife, unbelief; apéritif.

-iege, liege, siege; besiege, prestige.

-ield, field, shield, weald, wield, yield; afield;
battlefield, Chesterfield.

    Also: **-eal** + **-ed** (as in *healed*, etc.)

    Also: **-eel** + **-ed** (as in *peeled*, etc.)

-ien. See **-ean.**

-iend (-ēnd), fiend; archfiend.

Also: **-ean** + **-ed** (as in *cleaned*, etc.)

Also: **-een** + **-ed** (as in *careened*, etc.)

-iend (-ĕnd). See **-end**.

-ier (-ĭr). See **-eer**.

-ier (-īr). See **-ire**.

-ierce, Bierce, fierce, pierce, tierce; transpierce.

-iest. See **-east**.

-ieu. See **-ew**.

-ieve. See **-eave**.

-iew. See **-ew**.

-ieze. See **-ease**.

-if, biff, cliff, glyph, griff, if, jiff, miff, riff, Riff, skiff, sniff, stiff, tiff, whiff; bindlestiff, handkerchief, hieroglyph, hippogriff, neckerchief.

-ife, fife, knife, life, rife, strife, wife; alewife, fishwife, housewife, jackknife, midwife; afterlife, Duncan Phyfe.

-iff. See **-if**.

-iffed. See **-ift**.

-ift, drift, gift, lift, rift, shift, shrift, sift, swift, thrift; adrift, snowdrift, spendthrift, spindrift, uplift.

Also: **-iff** + **-ed** (as in *whiffed*, etc.)

-ig, big, brig, dig, fig, gig, grig, jig, pig, prig, rig, sprig, swig, trig, twig, Whig, wig; brillig, renege; infra dig, periwig, thimblerig, whirligig; thingumajig.

-igh. See **-y**.

-ighed. See **-ide**.

-ighs. See **-ize**.

-ight. See **-ite**.

-ign. See **-ine**.

-igned. See **-ind**.

-igue. See **-eague**.

-ike, bike, dike, hike, Ike, like, Mike, pike, psych, shrike, spike, tyke; alike, dislike, Klondike, oblique, turnpike, unlike, Vandyke; marlinspike.

-il. See **-ill.**

-ilch, filch, milch, pilch, Zilch.

-ild (-ĭld), build, gild, guild; rebuild, regild, unchilled, untilled; unfulfilled.
Also: **-ill** + **-ed** (as in *killed, skilled,* etc.)

-ild (-īld), aisled, child, mild, wild, Wilde.
Also: **-ile** + **-ed** (as in *filed,* etc.)
Also: **-yle** + **-ed** (as in *styled,* etc.)

-ile (-īl), aisle, bile, chyle, faille, file, guile, heil, I'll, isle, lisle, mile, Nile, pile, rile, smile, stile, style, tile, vile, while, wile; anile, Argyle, awhile, beguile, compile, defile, edile, erewhile, exile, gentile, meanwhile, revile, senile, servile; Anglophile, crocodile, domicile, Francophile, infantile, juvenile, mercantile, puerile, reconcile, Slavophile; aileurophile, bibliophile, Germanophile.

-ile (-ēl). See **-eal.**

-ile (-ĭl). See **-ill.**

-iled. See **-ild.**

-ilk, bilk, ilk, milk, silk.

-ill, bill, Bill, brill, chill, dill, drill, fill, frill, gill, grill, hill, ill, Jill, kill, mill, nil, Phil, pill, quill, rill, shill, shrill, sill, skill, spill, squill, still, swill, thill, thrill, 'til, till, trill, twill, 'twill, will, Will; Brazil, distil, downhill, fulfill, instill, quadrille, Seville, uphill; chlorophyll, codicil, daffodil, domicile, imbecile, Louisville, versatile, volatile, whippoorwill.

-ille (-ēl). See **-eal.**

-ille (-ĭl). See **-ill**.

-illed. See **-ild**.

-ilt, built, gilt, guilt, hilt, jilt, kilt, lilt, milt, quilt, silt, spilt, stilt, tilt, wilt; atilt, rebuilt; Vanderbilt.

-ilth, filth, spilth, tilth.

-im, brim, dim, glim, grim, Grimm, gym, him, hymn, Jim, Kim, limb, limn, prim, rim, shim, skim, slim, swim, Tim, trim, vim, whim; bedim, paynim, prelim; acronym, antonym, cherubim, eponym, homonym, interim, paradigm, pseudonym, seraphim, synonym.

-imb (-ĭm). See **-im**.

-imb (-īm). See **-ime**.

-ime, chime, chyme, climb, clime, crime, cyme, dime, grime, I'm, lime, mime, prime, rhyme, rime, slime, thyme, time; begrime, bedtime, berhyme, daytime, lifetime, meantime, some-time, springtime, sublime, upclimb; Guggen-heim, maritime, overtime, pantomime, paradigm, summertime, wintertime.

-imes, betimes, ofttimes, sometimes; often-times.

Also: **-ime** + **-s** (as in *crimes*, etc.)

Also: **-yme** + **-s** (as in *rhymes*, etc.)

-imp, blimp, chimp, crimp, gimp, guimpe, imp, limp, pimp, primp, scrimp, shrimp, simp, skimp.

-impse, glimpse.

Also: **-imp** + **-s** (as in *skimps*, etc.)

-in, been, bin, chin, din, djinn, fin, Finn, gin, grin, in, inn, jinn, kin, pin, shin, sin, skin, spin, thin, tin, twin, whin, win; akin, bear-

skin, begin, Berlin, bowfin, buckskin, carbine,
chagrin, Corinne, herein, sidespin, tailspin,
therein; alkaline, aniline, aquiline, aspirin,
crinoline, crystalline, discipline, feminine,
gelatin, genuine, glycerine, harlequin, hero-
ine, Jacobin, javelin, jessamine, mandarin,
mandolin, mannequin, masculine, Mickey
Finn, moccasin, paladin, peregrine, Rin-Tin-
Tin, saccharin, sibylline, violin, Zeppelin;
adrenalin, Alexandrine, elephantine.

-inc. See **-ink.**

-ince, blintz, chintz, mince, prince, quince, rinse,
since, wince; convince, evince.

Also: **-int** + **-s** (as in *prints*, etc.)

-inch, chinch, cinch, clinch, finch, flinch, inch,
lynch, pinch, winch; chaffinch, goldfinch.

-inct, tinct; distinct, extinct, instinct, precinct,
succinct.

Also: **-ink** + **-ed** (as in *winked*, etc.)

-ind (-īnd), bind, blind, find, grind, hind, kind,
mind, rind, wind; behind, mankind, purblind,
remind, unkind, unwind; colorblind, master-
mind, undersigned, womankind.

Also: **-ign** + **-ed** (as in *signed*, etc.)

Also: **-ine** + **-ed** (as in *dined*, etc.)

-ind (-ĭnd), Ind, wind; rescind; Amerind,
tamarind.

Also: **-in** + **-ed** (as in *grinned*, etc.)

-ine (-īn), brine, chine, dine, fine, kine, line,
mine, nine, pine, Rhine, shine, shrine, sign,
sine, spine, spline, stein, swine, syne, thine,
tine, trine, twine, vine, whine, wine; airline
align, assign, benign, bovine, canine, carbine,
carmine, combine, condign, confine, consign,

decline, define, design, divine, enshrine, entwine, feline, hircine, Holstein, incline, lifeline, malign, moonshine, opine, outshine, ovine, railline, recline, refine, repine, resign, saline, sunshine, supine, vulpine, woodbine; Adeline, alkaline, anodyne, Apennine, aquiline, Argentine, asinine, Byzantine, calcimine, calomine, Caroline, Clementine, columbine, concubine, disincline, eglantine, etamine, Florentine, interline, intertwine, iodine, leonine, Liechtenstein, palatine, porcupine, Proserpine, saturnine, serpentine, superfine, timberline, Turnverein, turpentine, underline, undermine, valentine, waterline; elephantine.

-ine (-ēn). See **-ean**.

-ine (-ĭn). See **-in**.

-ined. See **-ind**.

-ing, bing, bring, cling, ding, fling, king, Ming, ping, ring, sing, sling, spring, sting, string, swing, Synge, thing, wing, wring, ying; evening, hireling, mainspring, something, unsling, unstring; anything, atheling, everything, opening, underling.

Also: participles in **-ing** and gerunds (as *clamoring*, etc.)

-inge, binge, cringe, fringe, hinge, Inge, singe, springe, swinge, tinge, twinge; impinge, infringe, syringe, unhinge.

-ingue. See **-ang**.

-ink, blink, brink, chink, clink, drink, fink, ink, kink, link, mink, pink, rink, shrink, sink, skink, slink, stink, swink, think, wink, zinc; bethink, forethink, hoodwink; bobolink Humperdinck, interlink, tiddlywink.

-inked. See -inct.

-inks. See -inx.

-inned. See -ind.

-inse. See -ince.

-int, dint, flint, glint, Gynt, hint, lint, mint,
print, quint, splint, sprint, squint, stint, tint;
asquint, footprint, imprint, misprint, reprint,
spearmint; aquatint, peppermint, septuagint.

-inth, plinth; absinthe, Corinth; hyacinth,
labyrinth, terebinth.

-ints. See -ince.

-inx, jinx, lynx, minx, sphinx; larynx, methinks,
salpinx; tiddlywinks.

Also: **-ink** + **-s** (as in *thinks*, etc.)

-ip, blip, chip, clip, dip, drip, flip, grip, grippe,
gyp, hip, kip, lip, nip, pip, quip, rip, scrip,
ship, sip, skip, slip, snip, strip, tip, trip,
whip, yip, zip; airstrip, cowslip, equip, flag-
ship, harelip, horsewhip, lightship, outstrip,
transship, unzip; battleship, underlip,
weatherstrip.

Also: words with **-ship** as suffix (as *fellow-
ship, scholarship,* etc.)

-ipe, gripe, pipe, ripe, snipe, stipe, stripe, swipe,
tripe, type, wipe; bagpipe, blowpipe, horn-
pipe, pitchpipe, sideswipe, tintype, unripe,
windpipe; archetype, collotype, guttersnipe,
Linotype, Monotype, overripe, prototype;
Daguerreotype, electrotype, stereotype.

-ipse, eclipse, ellipse; apocalypse.

Also: **-ip** + **-s** (as in *chips*, etc.)

-ique. See -eak.

-ir. See -er.

-irch. See -urch.

-ird. See **-urd.**

-ire, bríar, brier, buyer, choir, dire, fire, flyer, friar, gyre, hire, ire, liar, lyre, mire, plier, prior, pyre, quire, shire, sire, spire, squire, tire, Tyre, wire; acquire, admire, afire, aspire, attire, bemire, bonfire, conspire, desire, empire, enquire, entire, esquire, expire, grandsire, inquire, inspire, perspire, quagmire, require, respire, retire, sapphire, satire, spitfire, transpire, wildfire.

Also: **-y** + **-er** (as in *crier, modifier,* etc.)

-irge. See **-erge.**

-irk. See **-urk.**

-irl. See **-url.**

-irm, berm, firm, germ, sperm, squirm, term, worm; affirm, confirm, glowworm, grubworm, infirm; isotherm, pachyderm.

-irp. See **-urp.**

-irr. See **-er.**

-irred. See **-urd.**

-irst. See **-urst.**

-irt. See **-ert.**

-irth, berth, birth, dearth, earth, firth, girth, mirth, Perth, worth; stillbirth, unearth.

-is (-ĭz), biz, fizz, friz, his, is, Liz, quiz, 'tis, viz, whiz, wiz; Cadiz.

-is (-ĭs). See **-iss.**

-ise (-īs). See **-ice.**

-ise (-īz). See **-ize.**

-ish, dish, fish, Gish, knish, pish, squish, swish, tish, wish; anguish, bluefish, flatfish, goldfish, whitefish, whitish; angelfish, babyish, devilfish, devilish, feverish, flying fish, gibberish, kittenish, womanish; impoverish.

-isk, bisque, brisk, disc, disk, frisk, risk, whisk;
asterisk, basilisk, obelisk, odalisque, tamarisk.

-ism, chrism, prism, schism; abysm, Babism,
baptism, Buddhism, Chartism, Comtism,
deism, faddism, Fascism, Grecism, Jainism,
Mahdism, monism, mutism, psellism, purism,
Scottism, snobbism, sophism, Sufism, tech-
nism, theism, Thomism, truism, Whiggism,
Yogism; absinthism, actinism, acrotism,
albinism, algorism, altruism, amorphism,
anarchism, aneurysm, Anglicism, animism,
aphorism, archaism, asterism, atavism, athe-
ism, atomism, Atticism, barbarism, Bentham-
ism, Biblicism, Bolshevism, Boswellism,
botulism, Brahminism, Briticism, Britishism,
brutalism, Byronism, cabalism, Caesarism,
Calvinism, carnalism, cataclysm, catechism,
Celticism, centralism, chauvinism, classicism,
cocainism, Cockneyism, Communism, cre-
tinism, criticism, cynicism, daltonism, dan-
dyism, Darwinism, demonism, despotism,
dimorphism, ditheism, dogmatism, dowdy-
ism, Druidism, dualism, dynamism, egoism,
egotism, embolism, Englishism, erethism,
ergotism, euphemism, euphonism, euphuism,
exorcism, extremism, fatalism, feminism,
fetishism, feudalism, fogyism, foreignism,
formalism, formulism, Gallicism, galvanism,
gentilism, Germanism, giantism, gigantism,
gnosticism, Gothicism, grundyism, heathen-
ism, Hebraism, hedonism, Hellenism, helot-
ism, heroism, Hinduism, Hitlerism, human-
ism, humorism, hypnotism, Irishism, Is-
lamism, Jansenism, jingoism, journalism,

Judaism, Junkerism, laconism, Lamaism, Lambdacism, Latinism, legalism, Leninism, localism, Lollardism, loyalism, magnetism, mannerism, martialism, masochism, mechanism, Menshevism, mephitism, mesmerism, Methodism, microcosm, Mithraism, modernism, monadism, moralism, Mormonism, morphinism, Mosaism, Moslemism, mysticism, narcotism, nepotism, nihilism, occultism, onanism, organism, optimism, ostracism, pacifism, paganism, pantheism, paroxysm, Parseeism, pauperism, pessimism, pietism, Platonism, pluralism, pragmatism, prognathism, prosaism, pyrrhonism, Quakerism, quietism, quixotism, Rabbinism, racialism, realism, regalism, rheumatism, Romanism, rowdyism, royalism, ruralism, satanism, Saxonism, schematism, scientism, Semitism, Shakerism, shamanism, Shintoism, sigmatism, Sinicism, skepticism, Socialism, solecism, solipsism, specialism, spiritism, spoonerism, Stalinism, stoicism, suffragism, syllogism, symbolism, synchronism, syncretism, synergism, tantalism, Taoism, terrorism, toadyism, Toryism, totemism, traumatism, tribalism, tritheism, ultraism, unionism, vandalism, verbalism, vocalism, volcanism, voodooism, vulgarism, vulpinism, witticism, Yankeeism, zealotism, Zionism; absenteeism, absolutism, achromatism, aestheticism, agnosticism, alcoholism, alienism, allotropism, amateurism, anabolism, anachronism, Anglicanism, antagonism, Arianism, asceticism, astigmatism, autochthonism, automatism, bimetallism, Byzantinism, cannibalism, capitalism, catabolism, Catholicism, charlatanism, clericalism, collectivism, commercialism, communalism, Confucianism, conservatism, democratism, determinism, diabolism, diletantism, eclecticism, empiricism, eroticism, Evangelism, expressionism, externalism, fanaticism, favoritism, federalism, generalism, Hibernicism, Hispanicism, hooliganism, hospitalism, hyperbolism, idealism, idiotism, impressionism, invalidism, isochronism, isomerism, isomorphism, isotropism, Jacobinism, Jacobitism, Jesuitism, katabolism, laconicism, legitimism, liberalism, libertinism, literalism, Lutheranism, malapropism, mercantilism, metabolism, metachronism, militarism, moderatism, monasticism, monotheism, mutualism, narcoticism, nationalism, naturalism, negativism, neologism, nicotinism, noctambulism, nominalism, objectivism, obscurantism, obstructionism, officialism, opportunism, parallelism, parasitism, paternalism, patriotism, pedagogism, Pharisaism, Philistinism, philosophism, plagiarism, plebianism, polymerism, polymorphism, polyphonism, polytheism, positivism, probabilism, progressivism, Protestantism, provincialism, Puritanism, radicalism, rationalism, recidivism, regionalism, ritualism, romanticism, ruffianism, Sadduceeism, scholasticism, secessionism, sectionalism, secularism, sensualism, separatism, Shavianism, somnambulism, somniloquism, subjectivism, sycophantism, syndicalism, theosophism, universalism, ventriloquism, Wesleyanism; abolitionism, agrarianism, Americanism, anthropomorphism, Bohemianism, Cartesianism, colloquialism, colonialism, conceptualism, conventionalism, cosmopolitism, equestrianism, evolutionism, existentialism, heliotropism, hermaphroditism, heteromorphism, Hibernianism, histrionicism, imperialism, incendiarism, indeterminism, indifferentism, industrialism, Manicheanism, materialism, medievalism, Mohammedanism, monometallism, Occidentalism, Orientalism, parochialism, phenomenalism, postimpressionism, professionalism, proverbialism, Republicanism, Rosicrucianism, sacerdotalism, sectarianism, sensationalism, sentimentalism, Spencerianism, spiritualism, theatricalism, Tractarianism, traditionalism, transmigrationism, Utopianism, vernacularism; antinomianism, antiquarianism, ceremonialism, Congregationalism, constitutionalism, cosmopolitanism, experimentalism, individualism, intellectualism, internationalism, presbyterianism, preternaturalism, proletarianism, supernaturalism, Unitarianism, vegetarianism; Aristotelianism, humanitarianism, utilitarianism; antidisestablishmentarianism.

-isp, crisp, lisp, wisp; will o' the wisp.

-iss, bliss, Chris, hiss, kiss, miss, Swiss, this; abyss, amiss, crevice, dismiss, jaundice, remiss, ywis; ambergris, armistice, artifice, avarice, Beatrice, benefice, chrysalis, cowardice, dentrifice, edifice, emphasis, genesis, nemesis, orifice, precipice, prejudice, synthesis, verdigris; acropolis, anabasis, analysis, antithesis, dieresis, hypothesis, metropolis, necropolis, paralysis, parenthesis, rigor mortis; metamorphosis; abiogenesis.

-ist (-ĭst), cist, cyst, fist, gist, grist, hist!, list, mist, schist, tryst, twist, whist, wist, wrist; artist, assist, Babist, Baptist, blacklist, Buddhist, chartist, chemist, Comtist, consist, Cubist, cueist, cyclist, deist, dentist, desist, druggist, duellist, enlist, entwist, exist, faddist, Fascist, flautist, florist, flutist, harpist, hymnist, insist, jurist, linguist, lutist, lyrist, metrist, monist, palmist, Papist, persist, psalmist, purist, resist, sacrist, simplist, sophist, statist, stylist, subsist, theist, Thomist, tourist, Trappist, tropist, typist, Yorkist; alarmist, alchemist, algebrist, Alpinist, altruist, amethyst, amorist, analyst, anarchist, animist, annalist, aorist, aphorist, Arabist, arbalest, archaist, archivist, armorist, atheist, atomist, balloonist, banjoist, biblicist, bicyclist, bigamist, Bolshevist, botanist, canoeist, cartoonist, casuist, catalyst, catechist, centralist, chauvinist, choralist, citharist, classicist, coexist, colloquist, colonist, colorist, Communist, conformist, copyist, Calvinist, cymbalist, Darwinist, diarist, dogmatist, Donatist, dramatist, dualist, egoist, egotist, elegist, essayist, Eucharist, eulogist, euphuist, extremist, fabulist, factionist, fatalist, fetishist, feudalist, fictionist, folklorist, formalist, futurist, guitarist, Hebraist, hedonist, Hellenist, herbalist, hobbyist, homilist, humanist, humorist, hypnotist,

intertwist, Jansenist, journalist, Judaist,
Lamaist, lampoonist, Latinist, legalist, Len-
inist, librettist, liturgist, lobbyist, loyalist,
machinist, martialist, mechanist, medallist,
mesmerist, Methodist, Mithraist, modernist,
monarchist, moralist, motorist, narcotist,
nepotist, Nihilist, novelist, occultist, oculist,
ophthalmist, optimist, organist, pacifist, pan-
theist, papalist, pessimist, pharmacist, physi-
cist, pianist, pietist, Platonist, pluralist,
portraitist, pragmatist, pre-exist, publicist,
pugilist, pyrrhonist, realist, re-enlist, reform-
ist, repealist, reservist, rhapsodist, Romanist,
ruralist, Sanskritist, satirist, scientist, sciolist,
Scripturist, Shamanist, Shintoist, Socialist,
solecist, soloist, specialist, Stalinist, strategist,
suffragist, symbolist, Talmudist, Taoist,
terrorist, theorist, trombonist, Trotskyist,
unionist, Vedantist, violist, vocalist, Zionist,
zitherist; abortionist, absolutist, accompan-
ist, agronomist, algebraist, alienist, Anabaptist, anatomist, antagonist, anthologist,
apiarist, apologist, astrologist, automatist,
autonomist, aviarist, bimetallist, biologist,
capitalist, chiropodist, clarinetist, clericalist,
collectivist, commercialist, communalist,
concessionist, conchologist, contortionist,
determinist, diplomatist, dramaturgist, econ-
omist, empiricist, enamelist, equilibrist,
Esperantist, ethnologist, Evangelist, exclu-
sionist, excursionist, expressionist, extor-
tionist, Federalist, geologist, geometrist,
horologist, hygienist, hyperbolist, idealist,
illusionist, impressionist, irredentist, legiti-

mist, liberalist, literalist, lycanthropist, manicurist, meliorist, metallurgist, militarist, misanthropist, misogamist, misogynist, monogamist, monologist, monopolist, monotheist, mosaicist, necrologist, negationist, negativist, neologist, neuropathist, noctambulist, Nominalist, nonconformist, objectivist, obscurantist, obstructionist, ocularist, opportunist, optometrist, panegyrist, parachutist, pathologist, perfectionist, philanthropist, philatelist, philogynist, phrenologist, plagiarist, polemicist, polygamist, pomologist, positivist, propagandist, protagonist, protectionist, psychiatrist, psychologist, psychopathist, rationalist, recidivist, religionist, revisionist, revivalist, ritualist, salvationist, secessionist, secularist, sensualist, separatist, soliloquist, somnambulist, somniloquist, spectroscopist, symbologist, syndicalist, synonymist, taxidermist, taxonomist, telepathist, telephonist, thaumaturgist, theologist, theosophist, therapeutist, tobacconist, traditionist, ventriloquist, violinist; abolitionist, agriculturist, anthropologist, anthropomorphist, archæologist, automobilist, caricaturist, coalitionist, conceptionalist, conceptualist, constitutionist, dermatologist, educationist, Egyptologist, elocutionist, embryologist, emigrationist, encyclopædist, entomologist, etymologist, evolutionist, federationist, floriculturist, genealogist, gynecologist, horticulturist, imperialist, insurrectionist, medievalist, melodramatist, mineralogist, miniaturist, monometallist,

Occidentalist, ophthalmologist, opposition-
ist, Orientalist, osteopathist, pharmacologist,
phenomenalist, physiologist, postimpression-
ist, preferentialist, prohibitionist, revolution-
ist, sacerdotalist, spiritualist, traditionalist,
transcendentalist, universalist, violoncellist;
vivisectionist; arboriculturist, Assyriologist,
bacteriologist, ceremonialist, Congregation-
alist, constitutionalist, controversialist,
conversationalist, educationalist, experimen-
talist, individualist, institutionalist, intel-
lectualist, internationalist, supernaturalist.

Also: **-iss** + **-ed** (as in *missed*, etc.)

-ist (-īst), Christ, feist; Zeitgeist.

Also: **-ice** + **-ed** (as in *sliced*, etc.)

-it, bit, bitt, chit, fit, flit, grit, hit, it, kit, knit, lit,
mitt, nit, pit, Pitt, quit, sit, skit, slit, smit,
spit, split, sprit, tit, twit, whit, wit, writ;
acquit, admit, armpit, befit, bowsprit, com-
mit, emit, misfit, moonlit, omit, outwit,
permit, refit, remit, respite, starlit, submit,
sunlit, titbit, tomtit, transmit, unfit; apposite,
benefit, counterfeit, definite, exquisite, favor-
ite, hypocrite, infinite, Jesuit, opposite,
perquisite, preterite, requisite; indefinite.

-itch, bitch, ditch, fitch, flitch, hitch, itch, niche,
pitch, rich, snitch, stitch, switch, twitch,
which, witch; bewitch, enrich, hemstitch,
unhitch; czarevich.

-ite (-īt), bight, bite, blight, bright, cite, dight,
Dwight, fight, flight, fright, height, hight,
kite, knight, light, might, mite, night, plight,
quite, right, rite, sight, site, sleight, slight,
smite, spite, sprite, tight, trite, white, wight,

wright, write; affright, alight, aright, bedight,
benight, contrite, daylight, delight, despite,
downright, dunnite, excite, foresight, forth-
right, goodnight, headlight, Hittite, hoplite,
ignite, incite, indict, indite, invite, midnight,
moonlight, outright, polite, recite, requite,
starlight, sunlight, tonight, twilight, unite,
upright, wainwright, wheelwright; acolyte,
aconite, anchorite, anthracite, appetite, blath-
erskite, Canaanite, candlelight, copyright,
disunite, dynamite, erudite, eremite, expedite,
fahrenheit, Gesundheit, impolite, Leninite,
Moabite, Muscovite, neophyte, overnight,
oversight, parasite, plebiscite, proselyte, rec-
ondite, satellite, stalactite, stalagmite, Stalin-
ite, troglodyte, Trotskyite, underwrite, vul-
canite, watersprite, watertight, weathertight,
Yemenite; electrolyte, gemütlichkeit, her-
maphrodite, Israelite, meteorite.

-ite (-ĭt). See **-it.**

-ites. See **-itz.**

-ith, frith, kith, myth, pith, smith, with; Edith,
forthwith, herewith, therewith, wherewith,
zenith; acrolith, Arrowsmith, monolith,
otolith.

-ithe, blithe, lithe, scythe, tithe, withe, writhe.

-itz, blitz, Fritz, grits, Ritz, spitz.

   Also: **-it** + **-s** (as in *bits*, etc.)

   Also: **-ite** + **-s** (as in *favorites*, etc.)

-ive (-īv), chive, Clive, dive, drive, five, gyve,
hive, I've, live, rive, shive, shrive, strive,
thrive, wive; alive, archive, arrive, beehive,
connive, contrive, deprive, derive, nosedive,
ogive, revive, survive; overdrive.

-ive (-ĭv), give, live, sieve, spiv; active, cap-
tive, costive, cursive, dative, fictive, forgive,
furtive, massive, missive, motive, native, out-
live, passive, pensive, plaintive, relive, restive,
sportive, suasive, votive; ablative, abortive,
abrasive, absorptive, abstersive, abstractive,
abusive, adaptive, additive, adductive, adhe-
sive, adjective, adjunctive, adoptive, affective,
afflictive, aggressive, allusive, amative, arres-
tive, aspersive, assertive, assuasive, assumptive, attentive, attractive, causative, coercive,
cognitive, cohesive, collective, collusive,
combative, combustive, compulsive, conative,
conceptive, concessive, concussive, conclusive, concoctive, conducive, conductive,
conflictive, congestive, conjunctive, connective, constrictive, constructive, consultive,
consumptive, contractive, convulsive, corrective, corrosive, corruptive, creative, curative,
deceptive, decisive, deductive, defective,
defensive, delusive, depictive, depressive,
derisive, descriptive, destructive, detective,
detractive, diffusive, digestive, digressive,
directive, discursive, disjunctive, disruptive,
dissuasive, distinctive, distractive, divertive,
divisive, divulsive, effective, effusive, elective,
elusive, emissive, emotive, emulsive, evasive,
excessive, exclusive, excursive, exhaustive,
expansive, expensive, expletive, explosive,
expressive, expulsive, extensive, extortive,
extractive, extrusive, fixative, formative,
fugitive, genitive, gerundive, hortative, illusive, impassive, impressive, impulsive, inactive, incentive, incisive, inclusive, incursive,

inductive, infective, inflective, infusive, ingestive, inscriptive, instinctive, instructive, intensive, intrusive, invective, inventive, laudative, laxative, lenitive, locative, lucrative, narrative, negative, nutritive, objective, obstructive, obtrusive, offensive, olfactive, oppressive, optative, partitive, perceptive, percussive, perfective, permissive, perspective, persuasive, pervasive, positive, possessive, preclusive, precursive, predictive, prescriptive, presumptive, preventive, primitive, privative, productive, progressive, projective, propulsive, proscriptive, prospective, protective, protractive, protrusive, punitive, purgative, purposive, reactive, receptive, recessive, redemptive, reductive, reflective, reflexive, regressive, relative, remissive, repressive, repulsive, respective, responsive, restrictive, resumptive, retentive, retractive, revulsive, secretive, sedative, seductive, selective, sensitive, siccative, subjective, subjunctive, submissive, substantive, subtractive, subversive, successive, suggestive, suppressive, talkative, tentative, transgressive, transitive, transmissive, vibrative, vindictive, vocative; abrogative, accusative, acquisitive, admonitive, adumbrative, affirmative, alternative, appellative, attributive, augmentative, calculative, carminative, circumscriptive, circumventive, coextensive, combinative, comparative, compensative, competitive, compositive, comprehensive, connotative, consecutive, conservative, contemplative, contributive, conversative, corporative, cor-

relative, corresponsive, counteractive, cumulative, declarative, decorative, dedicative,
definitive, demonstrative, denotative, depre-
cative, derivative, diminutive, disputative,
distributive, educative, evocative, excitative,
exclamative, execrative, executive, exhibitive,
exhortative, expectative, explicative, explora-
tive, expositive, figurative, generative, germi-
native, hesitative, illustrative, imitative,
imperative, imperceptive, inattentive, inco-
hesive, inconclusive, indecisive, indicative,
indistinctive, ineffective, inexhaustive, inex-
pansive, inexpensive, inexpressive, infinitive,
informative, innovative, inoffensive, inquisi-
tive, insensitive, integrative, intransitive,
introductive, introspective, intuitive, irrespective, irresponsive, irritative, iterative,
judicative, legislative, locomotive, mediative
medicative, meditative, nominative, operative, palliative, pejorative, perforative,
preparative, prerogative, preservative, pre-
ventative, procreative, prohibitive, provoca-
tive, putrefactive, qualitative, quantitative,
radiative, rarefactive, reconstructive, recre-
ative, regulative, remonstrative, repetitive,
reprehensive, reprobative, reproductive, retroactive, retrogressive, retrospective, rumi-
native, segregative, speculative, stupefactive,
superlative, suppurative, vegetative, vindica-
tive; accumulative, administrative, agglutina-
tive, alleviative, alliterative, appreciative,
argumentative, assimilative, associative,
authoritative, coagulative, commemorative,
commiserative, communicative, conciliative,

confederative, cooperative, corroborative, deliberative, depreciative, discriminative, exonerative, expostulative, imaginative, initiative, inoperative, interpretative, interrogative, investigative, irradiative, manipulative, recuperative, reiterative, remunerative, representative, retaliative, significative, subordinative, vituperative; incommunicative, philoprogenitive.

-ix, fix, mix, nix, pyx, six, Styx; admix, affix, commix, infix, matrix, onyx, prefix, prolix, suffix, transfix, unfix; cicatrix, crucifix, fiddlesticks, intermix, politics; executrix; archæopteryx.

Also: **-ick + -s** (as in *bricks*, *sticks*, etc.)

-ixed. See **-ixt.**

-ixt, twixt; betwixt.

Also: **-ix + -ed** (as in *mixed*, etc.)

-iz. See **-is.**

-ize, guise, prize, rise, size, wise; advise, apprise, arise, assize, baptize, capsize, chastise, cognize, comprise, demise, despise, devise, disguise, incise, likewise, misprize, moonrise, revise, sunrise, surmise, surprise, unwise; advertise, aggrandize, agonize, alkalize, amortize, Anglicize, atomize, authorize, barbarize, bastardize, bowdlerize, brutalize, canalize, canonize, carbonize, catechize, cauterize, centralize, circumcise, civilize, classicize, colonize, compromise, criticize, crystallize, deputize, dogmatize, dramatize, emphasize, energize, enterprise, equalize, eulogize, euphemize, exercise, exorcise, feminize, fertilize, feudalize, focalize, formalize, fossilize, fractionize, fraternize, Gallicize, galvanize, Germanize, glutinize, harmonize, Hellenize, humanize, hybridize, hypnotize, idolize, immunize, improvise, ionize, itemize, jeopardize, Judaize, laicize, Latinize, legalize, lionize, liquidize, localize, magnetize, martyrize, maximize, mechanize, memorize, mercerize, mesmerize, metallize, methodize, minimize, mobilize, modernize, monetize, moralize, nasalize, neutralize, normalize, organize, ostracize, otherwise, oxidize, patronize, penalize, pluralize, polarize, polemize, pulverize, realize, recognize, rhapsodize, Romanize, ruralize, Russianize, satirize, scandalize, schematize, scrutinize, sermonize, signalize, socialize, solemnize, specialize, stabilize, standardize, sterilize, stigmatize, subsidize, summarize, supervise, symbolize, sympathize, symphonize, synchronize, synthesize, systemize, tantalize, televise, temporize, terrorize, theorize, totalize, tranquilize, tyrannize, unionize, utilize, vaporize, verbalize, victimize, vitalize, vocalize, vulcanize, vulgarize, Westernize; acclimatize, actualize, allegorize, alphabetize, anæsthetize, anatomize, antagonize, anthologize, apologize, apostatize, apostrophize, capitalize, catholicize, characterize, Christianize, circularize, commercialize, decentralize, dehumanize, demobilize, democratize, demonetize, demoralize, deodorize, disorganize, economize, epitomize, extemporize, federalize, generalize, hydrogenize, hypothesize, idealize, immobilize, immortalize, italicize, legitimize, liberalize, metabolize,

militarize, monopolize, nationalize, natural-
ize, parenthesize, personalize, philosophize,
plagiarize, popularize, proselytize, rational-
ize, regularize, reorganize, ritualize, singu-
larize, skeletonize, soliloquize, systematize,
theologize, theosophize, visualize, ventrilo-
quize; Americanize, anathematize, apotheo-
size, departmentalize, etymologize, familiarize,
legitimatize, materialize, memorialize, partic-
ularize, professionalize, republicanize, revolu-
tionize, secularize, sentimentalize, spiritualize,
universalize; constitutionalize, individualize,
institutionalize, intellectualize, internation-
alize.

Also: **-y** + **-s** (as in *testifies*, etc.)

Also: **-eye** + **-s** (as in *eyes*, etc.)

Also: **-igh** + **-s** (as in *sighs*, etc.)

-o (-ō). See **-ow.**

-o (-ōō). See **-oo.**

-oach, broach, brooch, coach, loach, poach,
roach; abroach, approach, cockroach, en-
croach, reproach.

-oad (-ôd). See **-aud.**

-oad (-ōd). See **-ode.**

-oaf, loaf, oaf.

-oak. See **-oke.**

-oaks. See **-oax.**

-oal. See **-ole.**

-oaled. See **-old.**

-oam. See **-ome.**

-oan. See **-one.**

-oap. See **-ope.**

-oar. See **-ore.**

-oard. See **-ord.**

-oared. See **-ord.**

-oast. See **-ost.**

-oat. See **-ote.**

-oath. See **-oth.**

-oax, coax, hoax.

    Also: **-oak** + **-s** (as in *cloaks*, etc.)

    Also: **-oke** + **-s** (as in *jokes*, etc.)

-ob, blob, bob, Bob, cob, Cobb, fob, glob, gob, hob, job, knob, lob, mob, nob, rob, slob, snob, sob, squab, swab, throb; cabob, hobnob, nabob; thingumbob.

-obe, globe, Job, lobe, probe, robe; conglobe, disrobe, enrobe, unrobe; Anglophobe, Francophobe, Gallophobe, Russophobe, Slavophobe.

-ock, Bach, Bloch, block, bock, chock, clock, cock, crock, doc, dock, flock, frock, hock, jock, Jock, knock, loch, lock, Mach, mock, pock, roc, rock, shock, smock, sock, stock; ad hoc, Bankok, deadlock, Dvořak, fetlock, Hancock, hemlock, padlock, peacock, petcock, Rorschach, shamrock, Sherlock, Shylock, tick-tock, unfrock, unlock, woodcock; alpenstock, Antioch, hollyhock, Jabberwock, poppycock, shuttlecock, weathercock.

-ocked. See **-oct.**

-ocks. See **-ox.**

-oct, concoct, decoct; shell-shocked.

    Also: **-ock** + **-ed** (as in *flocked*, etc.)

-od, clod, cod, God, hod, nod, odd, plod, pod, prod, quad, quod, rod, scrod, shod, sod, squad, tod, trod, wad; ballade, couvade, facade, roughshod, roulade, slipshod, unshod, untrod; decapod, demigod, goldenrod, lycopod, promenade.

-ode, bode, code, goad, load, lode, mode, node, ode, road, rode, Spode, strode, toad, woad; abode, anode, cathode, commode, corrode, erode, explode, implode, forebode, railroad, reload, unload; à la mode, discommode, episode, overload, pigeon-toed.

Also: **-ow** + **-ed** (as in *towed*, etc.)

-odge, dodge, hodge, lodge, podge, stodge; dislodge, hodgepodge.

-oe (-ō). See **-ow.**

-oe (-o͞o). See **-ew.**

-oes (-ōz). See **-ose.**

-oes (-ŭz). See **-uzz.**

-off, cough, doff, off, scoff, soph, trough; Khrushchev, takeoff; philosophe. See also **-aff.**

-offed. See **-oft.**

-oft, croft, loft, oft, soft; aloft, hayloft.

Also: **-off** + **-ed** (as in *doffed*, etc.)

Also: **-ough** + **-ed** (as in *coughed*, etc.)

-og, bog, clog, cog, dog, flog, fog, frog, grog, hog, jog, log, nog, Prague, slog; agog, bulldog, eggnog, incog, unclog; analogue, catalogue, decalogue, demagogue, dialogue, epilogue, monologue, pedagogue, pettifog, synagogue, travelogue.

-ogue (-ōg). brogue, rogue, vogue; prorogue; disembogue.

-ogue (-ŏg). See **-og.**

-oice, choice, Joyce, voice; invoice, rejoice, Rolls Royce.

-oiced. See **-oist.**

-oid, Floyd, Freud, Lloyd, void; avoid, devoid, Negroid, ovoid, tabloid; alkaloid, aneroid, anthropoid, asteroid, celluloid, Mongoloid, trapezoid; paraboloid.

Also: **-oy** + **-ed** (as in *enjoyed*, etc.)

-oil, boil, broil, coil, foil, Hoyle, moil, oil, roil, soil, spoil, toil; despoil, embroil, gumboil, parboil, recoil, tinfoil, trefoil, turmoil, uncoil.

-oin, coign, coin, groin, join, loin, quoin; adjoin, benzoin, Burgoyne, conjoin, Des Moines, disjoin, enjoin, purloin, rejoin, sirloin, subjoin; tenderloin.

-oint, joint, point; anoint, appoint, aroint, conjoint, disjoint, dry-point, West Point; counterpoint, disappoint.

-oise, noise, poise; counterpoise, equipoise, Illinois, Iroquois; avoirdupois.

Also: **-oy** + **-s** (as in *toys*, etc.)

-oist, foist, hoist, joist, moist.

Also: **-oice** + **-ed** (as in *voiced*, etc.)

-oit, coit, doit, quoit; adroit, Beloit, dacoit, Detroit, exploit, introit; maladroit.

-oke, bloke, broke, choke, cloak, coke, Coke, croak, folk, joke, oak, oke, poke, smoke, soak, spoke, stoke, stroke, toque, woke, yoke, yolk; awoke, baroque, bespoke, convoke, evoke, invoke, provoke, revoke; artichoke, counterstroke, gentlefolk, masterstroke.

-okes. See **-oax.**

-ol (-ŏl), doll, loll, moll, Sol; atoll; alcohol, capitol, folderol, parasol, protocol, vitriol.

-ol (-ōl). See **-ole.**

-old, bold, cold, fold, gold, hold, mold, mould,

old, scold, sold, told, wold; behold, blindfold,
cuckold, enfold, foothold, foretold, freehold,
household, retold, stronghold, threshold,
toehold, twofold, unfold, untold, uphold,
withhold; manifold, marigold, overbold.

Also: **-oal** + **-ed** (as in *foaled*, etc.)

Also: **-ole** + **-ed** (as in *paroled*, etc.)

Also: **-oll** + **-ed** (as in *rolled*, etc.)

-ole, bole, boll, bowl, coal, dole, droll, foal,
goal, hole, Joel, knoll, kohl, mole, pole, poll,
role, roll, scroll, shoal, skoal, sole, soul,
stole, stroll, thole, toll, troll, whole; cajole,
condole, console, control, Creole, enroll,
flagpole, loophole, Maypole, parole, patrol,
payroll, peephole, petrol; aerosol, Anatole,
barcarole, buttonhole, camisole, girandole,
girasole, oriole, rigmarole, rock 'n' roll,
Seminole; filet of sole.

-oled. See **-old.**

-olk. See **-oke.**

-oll (-ŏl). See **-ol.**

-oll (-ōl). See **-ole.**

-olled. See **-old.**

-olt, bolt, colt, dolt, holt, jolt, molt, poult,
volt; revolt, unbolt; thunderbolt.

-olve, solve; absolve, convolve, devolve, dis-
solve, evolve, involve, resolve, revolve.

-om (-ŏm), bomb, dom, from, prom, rhomb,
Tom; aplomb, pogrom, pompom, therefrom,
wherefrom.

-om (-ōōm). See **-oom.**

-omb (-ŏm). See **-om.**

-omb (-ōm). See **-ome.**

-omb (-ōōm). See **-oom.**

-ome (-ōm), chrome, comb, dome, foam, gnome, holm, home, loam, mome, Nome, ohm, roam, Rome, tome; aplomb, cockscomb, coulomb, Jerome; aerodrome, catacomb, currycomb, gastronome, hippodrome, honeycomb, metronome, monochrome, palindrome.

-ome (-ŭm). See **-um**.

-omp, comp, pomp, romp, swamp.

-ompt, prompt, romped, swamped.

-on (-ŏn), con, don, gone, John, on, scone, swan, wan, yon; anon, Argonne, Aswan, begone, bonbon, bygone, Ceylon, chiffon, cretonne, hereon, icon, neutron, proton, thereon, upon, Yvonne; Algernon, Amazon, antiphon, Aragon, Avalon, betatron, bevatron, colophon, decagon, deuteron, echelon, electron, epsilon, Helicon, hexagon, lexicon, Marathon, marathon, mastodon, mesotron, myrmidon, nonagon, octagon, omicron, Oregon, paragon, Parthenon, Pentagon, polygon, Rubicon, silicon, synchrotron, tarragon, upsilon; phenomenon, Saskatchewan; prolegomenon; parallelopipedon.

-on (-ŭn). See **-un**.

-once (-ŏns), Hans, nonce, sconce, wants; ensconce, response, séance; liederkranz.

Also: **-aunt** + **-s** (as in *taunts*, etc.)

-once (-ŭns). See **-unce**.

-onch. See **-onk**.

-ond, blond, blonde, bond, fond, frond, pond, wand, yond; abscond, beyond, despond, respond; correspond, demimonde, vagabond.

Also: **-on** + **-ed** (as in *donned*, etc.)

-one (-ōn), bone, blown, cone, crone, drone,

flown, groan, grown, hone, Joan, known,
loan, lone, moan, mohn, mown, own, phone,
pone, prone, roan, Rhone, scone, shone,
shown, sown, stone, throne, thrown, tone,
zone; alone, atone, backbone, Bayonne,
bemoan, brimstone, cologne, Cologne, con-
done, curbstone, depone, dethrone, disown,
enthrone, flagstone, grindstone, headstone,
intone, keystone, milestone, millstone, moon-
stone, ozone, postpone, trombone, unknown,
unsewn; baritone, chaperone, cicerone, cor-
nerstone, dictaphone, ediphone, gramaphone,
megaphone, microphone, monotone, over-
grown, overthrown, saxophone, telephone,
undertone, xylophone.

-one (-ŏn). See **-on**.

-one (-ŭn). See **-un**.

-ong (-ŏng), gong, long, prong, song, strong,
thong, throng, tong, Tong, wrong; along,
belong, dingdong, diphthong, dugong, head-
long, headstrong, Hongkong, King Kong,
lifelong, mahjongg, oblong, pingpong, pro-
long, souchong; evensong, overlong.

-ong (-ŭng). See **-ung**.

-ongue. See **-ung.**

-onk (-ŏnk), conch, conk, honk.

-onk (-ŭnk). See **-unk.**

-onned. See **-ond.**

-onse. See **-once.**

-ont (-ŏnt), font, want; Vermont; Hellespont.

-ont (-ŭnt). See **-unt.**

-oo. See **-ew.**

-ood (-o͞od), could, good, hood, should, stood,
wood, would; childhood, firewood, man-

hood, monkshood, withstood; babyhood,
brotherhood, fatherhood, hardihood, Holly-
wood, likelihood, livelihood, maidenhood,
motherhood, neighborhood, parenthood,
Robin Hood, sandalwood, sisterhood, under-
stood, womanhood; misunderstood.

-ood (-o͞od). See **-ude.**

-oof, goof, hoof, pouf, proof, roof, spoof, woof;
aloof, behoof, disproof, fireproof, rainproof,
reproof, Tartuffe; waterproof, weatherproof;
opera bouffe.

-ook (-o͝ok), book, brook, cook, crook, hook,
look, nook, rook, shook, took; betook,
Chinook, forsook, mistook, nainsook, out-
look, partook; overlook, pocketbook, under-
took.

-ook (-o͞ok). See **-uke.**

-ool, cool, drool, fool, ghoul, pool, rule,
school, spool, stool, tool, tulle, who'll;
ampoule, befool, footstool, home rule, mis-
rule, toadstool whirlpool; Istanbul, Liver-
pool, overrule.

See also **-ule.**

-oom, bloom, boom, broom, brume, doom,
flume, fume, gloom, groom, loom, plume,
rheum, room, spume, tomb, whom, womb;
abloom, assume, bridegroom, consume, cos-
tume, entomb, exhume, Fiume, heirloom,
illume, Khartoum, legume, perfume, pre-
sume, relume, resume, simoom, subsume;
anteroom, hecatomb, reassume.

-oon, boon, Boone, coon, croon, dune, goon,
hewn, June, loon, moon, noon, prune, rune,
soon, spoon, swoon, tune; attune, baboon,

balloon, bassoon, bestrewn, buffoon, cartoon, cocoon, commune, doubloon, dragoon, eftsoon, festoon, forenoon, galloon, harpoon, high noon, immune, impugn, jejune, lagoon, lampoon, maroon, midnoon, monsoon, oppugn, platoon, poltroon, pontoon, quadroon, raccoon, Rangoon, Simoon, spittoon, tycoon, typhoon, Walloon; afternoon, brigadoon, Cameroun, honeymoon, importune, macaroon, octoroon, opportune, pantaloon, picaroon, picayune, rigadoon.

-ooned. See **-ound.**

-oop, coop, croup, droop, drupe, dupe, goop, group, hoop, jupe, Krupp, loop, poop, scoop, sloop, soup, stoop, stoup, stupe, swoop, troop, troupe, whoop; recoup; Guadeloupe, nincompoop.

-oor (-ōor), boor, brewer, dour, moor, poor, Ruhr, sewer, spoor, sure, tour, Ur; abjure, adjure, amour, assure, brochure, contour, detour, ensure, insure, tonsure, unsure; blackamoor, cynosure, Kohinoor, paramour, petit four, reassure; affaire d'amour. See also **-ure.**

-oor (-ôr). See **-ore.**

-oors. See **-ours.**

-oose (-ōōs), Bruce, deuce, goose, juice, loose, moose, noose, puce, sluice, spruce, truce, use, Zeus; abduce, abstruse, abuse, adduce, burnoose, caboose, conduce, deduce, diffuse, disuse, excuse, induce, misuse, obtuse, papoose, produce, profuse, recluse, reduce, seduce, Toulouse, traduce, vamoose; cala-

boose, charlotte russe, introduce, reproduce,
Syracuse; hypotenuse.

-oose (-ōōz). See **-ooze**.

-oosed. See **-oost**.

-oost, boost, deuced, Proust, roost.

Also: **-uce** + **-ed** (as in *reduced*, etc.)

Also: **-oose** + **-ed** (as in *loosed*, etc.)

-oot (-ōōt), boot, bruit, brute, chute, coot,
flute, fruit, hoot, jute, loot, moot, root, route,
shoot, skoot, toot; Beirut, cahoot, Canute,
cheroot, galloot, recruit, uproot; Aleut,
bandicoot, bumbershoot, overshoot, para-
chute. See also **-ute**.

-oot (-ŏŏt), foot, put, soot; afoot, forefoot,
hotfoot, input, output; pussyfoot, underfoot;
tenderfoot.

-ooth (-ōōth), booth, couth, ruth, Ruth, sleuth,
sooth, tooth, truth, youth; Duluth, forsooth,
uncouth, vermouth.

-oothe (-ōōth̶), smooth, soothe.

-oove. See **-ove**.

-ooze, blues, booze, bruise, choose, cruise, lose,
ooze, ruse, shoes, snooze, who's, whose;
peruse; Betelgeuse. See also **-use**.

Also: **-ew** + **-s** (as in *chews*, etc.)

Also: **-oo** + **-s** (as in *moos*, etc.)

Also: **-ue** + **-s** (as in *dues*, etc.)

-op, bop, chop, cop, crop, drop, flop, fop, hop,
lop, mop, plop, pop, prop, shop, slop, sop,
stop, strop, swap, top; Aesop, atop, co-op,
dewdrop, eavesdrop, estop, flipflop, snow-
drop, tiptop, workshop; aftercrop, lollipop,
Malaprop, overstop, whistle-stop.

-ope, cope, dope, grope, hope, lope, mope,

nope, ope, pope, rope, scope, slope, soap,
taupe, tope, trope; elope; antelope, antipope,
cantaloupe, envelope, gyroscope, horoscope,
interlope, isotope, microscope, misanthrope,
periscope, stethoscope, telescope; heliotrope,
kaleidoscope.

-opped. See **-opt.**

-opt, copt, opt; adopt.

Also: **-op** + **-ed** (as in *topped*, etc.)

-or (-ôr), for, lor, nor, or, Thor, tor, war;
abhor, bailor, donor, furor, junior, lessor,
senior, señor, vendor; ancestor, auditor,
bachelor, chancellor, conqueror, corridor,
creditor, counselor, cuspidor, dinosaur, Ecua-
dor, editor, emperor, governor, guarantor,
janitor, Labrador, matador, metaphor, me-
teor, minotaur, monitor, orator, picador,
Salvador, senator, troubadour, visitor, war-
rior; ambassador, competitor, compositor,
conspirator, contributor, depositor, executor,
ichthyosaur, inheritor, inquisitor, progenitor,
proprietor, solicitor, toreador. See also **-ore.**

-or (-ōr). See **-ore.**

-orb, orb; absorb.

-orce. See **-orse.**

-orch, porch, scorch, torch.

-ord, board, chord, cord, fiord, ford, Ford,
gourd, hoard, horde, lord, sward, sword,
toward, ward; aboard, abhorred, accord,
afford, award, broadsword, concord, discord,
landlord, record, reward, seaboard, unto-
ward; clavichord, harpsichord.

Also: **-oar** + **-ed** (as in *roared*, etc.)

Also: **-ore** + **-ed** (as in *scored*, etc.)

-ore, boar, Boer, bore, chore, core, corps, door, floor, fore, frore, four, gore, hoar, lore, more, oar, o'er, ore, pore, pour, roar, score, shore, snore, soar, sore, store, swore, tore, whore, wore, yore; adore, afore, ashore, before, claymore, deplore, encore, explore, folklore, footsore, forbore, forswore, galore, heartsore, ignore, implore, restore; albacore, battledore, Baltimore, commodore, evermore, furthermore, hellebore, heretofore, nevermore, pinafore, sagamore, semaphore, Singapore, sophomore, stevedore, sycamore, underscore. See also **-or.**

-ored. See **-ord.**

-orge, forge, George, gorge; disgorge, engorge, regorge.

-ork, cork, Cork, fork, pork, stork, torque, York; New York, pitchfork, uncork.

-orld, world.
   Also: **-url** + **-ed** (as in *curled,* etc.)

-orm, corm, dorm, form, norm, storm, swarm, warm; conform, deform, inform, misform, perform, reform, snowstorm, transform; chloroform, cruciform, misinform, multiform, thunderstorm, uniform, vermiform; cuneiform, iodoform.

-orn, born, borne, bourn, corn, horn, lorn, morn, mourn, scorn, shorn, sworn, thorn, torn, warn, worn; acorn, adorn, blackthorn, buckthorn, first-born, foghorn, forewarn, forlorn, forsworn, greenhorn, hawthorn, Leghorn, lovelorn, outworn, popcorn, stillborn, suborn, toilworn, unborn; alpenhorn,

barleycorn, Capricorn, Matterhorn, pepper-
corn, unicorn, yestermorn.

-orp, dorp, thorp, warp.

-orse, coarse, corse, course, force, gorse, hoarse,
horse, Morse, Norse, source, torse; con-
course, discourse, divorce, endorse, enforce,
perforce, recourse, remorse, resource, sea-
horse, unhorse; hobbyhorse, intercourse,
reinforce, watercourse.

-orst. See **-urst.**

-ort, bort, court, fort, forte, mort, ort,
port, quart, short, snort, sort, sport, swart,
thwart, tort, wart; abort, assort, athwart,
cavort, cohort, comport, consort, contort,
deport, disport, distort, escort, exhort, export,
extort, import, passport, purport, rapport,
report, resort, retort, seaport, transport.

-orts. See **-artz.**

-orth, forth, fourth, north, swarth; henceforth,
thenceforth.

-ose (-ōs), close, dose, gross; engross, globose,
glucose, jocose, morose, verbose; acerose,
adipose, bellicose, cellulose, comatose, diag-
nose, grandiose, otiose, overdose.

-ose (-ōz), chose, close, clothes, doze, froze,
gloze, hose, nose, pose, prose, rose, Rose,
those; Ambrose, arose, compose, depose,
disclose, dispose, enclose, expose, foreclose,
impose, inclose, oppose, propose, repose,
suppose, transpose, unclose, unfroze; decom-
pose, discompose, indispose, interpose, pre-
dispose, presuppose, tuberose, twinkle-toes.
Also: **-o** + **-s** (as in *punctilios*, etc.)
Also: **-o** + **-es** (as in *goes*, etc.)

Also -oe + -s (as in *toes*, etc.)

Also: -ot + -s (as in *depots*, etc.)

Also: -ow + -s (as in *glows*, etc.)

-osk, bosk, mosque; kiosk.

-osque. See **-osk.**

-oss, boss, cos, cross, dross, floss, fosse, gloss, hoss, joss, loss, moss, os, Ross, sauce, toss; across, emboss, lacrosse, reredos; albatross, applesauce; rhinoceros.

-ost (-ôst or -ŏst), cost, frost, lost, wast; accost, exhaust; holocaust, Pentecost.

Also: **-oss** + **-ed** (as in *tossed*, etc.)

-ost (-ōst), boast, coast, ghost, grossed, host, most, oast, post, roast, toast; almost, engrossed, foremost, hindmost, riposte, seacoast, signpost; aftermost, furthermost, hindermost, hitching post, innermost, lowermost, nethermost, outermost, undermost, uppermost, uttermost.

-ot, blot, clot, cot, dot, Dot, got, grot, hot, jot, knot, lot, not, plot, pot, rot, scot, Scot, shot, slot, snot, sot, spot, squat, tot, trot, watt, what, wot, yacht; allot, begot, besot, boycott, cocotte, culotte, dogtrot, ergot, forgot, foxtrot, fylfot, garotte, gavotte, grapeshot, kumquat, loquat, somewhat, unknot; Aldershot, aliquot, apricot, bergamot, Camelot, counterplot, eschalot, gallipot, Hottentot, Huguenot, Lancelot, misbegot, patriot, polyglot, tommyrot, unbegot, undershot; forget-me-not.

-otch, blotch, botch, crotch, notch, scotch, Scotch, splotch, swatch, watch; hopscotch, hotchpotch, topnotch.

-ote, bloat, boat, Choate, coat, cote, dote,
float, gloat, goat, groat, moat, mote, note,
oat, quote, rote, shoat, smote, stoat, throat,
tote, vote, wrote; afloat, capote, connote,
demote, denote, devote, emote, footnote,
lifeboat, misquote, outvote, promote, remote,
steamboat, topcoat, unquote; anecdote, anti-
dote, asymptote, billygoat, creosote, nanny
goat, overcoat, petticoat, redingote, table
d'hôte; witenagemot.

-oth (-ôth), broth, cloth, froth, Goth, moth,
swath, Thoth, troth, wroth; betroth, broad-
cloth, sackcloth; Ashtaroth, behemoth,
Ostrogoth, Visigoth.

-oth (-ōth), both, growth, loath, oath, quoth,
sloth, wroth; overgrowth, undergrowth.

-othe, clothe, loathe; betroth.

-ou (-ou). See **-ow.**

-ou (-ū). See **-ew.**

-oubt. See **-out.**

-ouch (-ouch), couch, crouch, groucn, ouch,
pouch, slouch, vouch; avouch.

-ouch (-ŭch). See **-utch.**

-ouche, douche, ruche; barouche, cartouche,
debouch; scaramouch.

-oud, cloud, crowd, loud, proud, shroud; aloud,
becloud, enshroud, o'ercloud; overcloud,
overcrowd, thundercloud.
Also: **-ow** + **-ed** (as in *bowed*, etc.)

-ough (-ôf). See **-off.**

-ough (-ou or -ō). See **-ow.**

-ough (-ŭf). See **-uff.**

-oughed. See **-oft.**

-ought, aught, bought, brought, caught, fought,

fraught, naught, nought, ought, sought, taught, taut, thought, wrought; besought, Connaught, distraught, dreadnought, forethought, methought, onslaught; aeronaut, afterthought, Argonaut, astronaut, Juggernaut, overwrought.

-oul (-oul). See **-owl**.

-oul (-ōl). See **-ole**.

-ould. See **-ood**.

-oun. See **-own**.

-ounce, bounce, flounce, frounce, ounce, pounce, trounce; announce, denounce, enounce, pronounce, renounce.

Also: **-ount** + **-s** (as in *counts*, etc.)

-ound (-ound), bound, found, ground, hound, mound, pound, round, sound, wound; abound, aground, around, astound, background, bloodhound, compound, confound, dumfound, expound, hidebound, homebound, horehound, icebound, inbound, outbound, profound, propound, rebound, redound, resound, spellbound, snowbound, surround, unbound, unfound; underground; merry-go-round.

Also: **-own** + **-ed** (as in *clowned*, etc.)

-ound (-ōōnd), wound.

Also: **-oon** + **-ed** (as in *swooned*, etc.)

Also: **-une** + **-ed** (as in *tuned*, etc.)

-ount, count, fount, mount; account, amount, discount, dismount, miscount, recount, remount, surmount; catamount, paramount, tantamount.

-ounts. See **-ounce**.

-oup. See **-oop**.

-our, bower, cower, dour, dower, flour, flower, glower, hour, lour, lower, our, power, scour, shower, sour, tower; deflower, devour, embower, empower, horsepower, manpower, sunflower, wallflower; Adenauer, cauliflower, Eisenhower, overpower.

Also: -ow + -er (as in *plower*, etc.)

-ourge. See -erge.

-ourn (-ôrn). See -orn.

-ourn (-ûrn). See -urn.

-ours (-ourz), ours.

Also: -our + -s (as in *devours*, etc.)

Also: -ower + -s (as in *flowers*, etc.)

-ours (-ŏŏrz), yours.

Also: -oor + -s (as in *boors*, etc.)

Also: -our + -s (as in *amours*, etc.)

Also: -ure + -s (as in *lures*, etc.)

-ourse. See -orse.

-ourt. See -ort.

-ourth. See -orth.

-ous. See -us.

-ouse, blouse, douse, grouse, house, louse, mouse, souse, spouse, Strauss; backhouse, birdhouse, clubhouse, delouse, doghouse, hothouse, jailhouse, madhouse, outhouse, penthouse, poorhouse, roundhouse, storehouse, warehouse, workhouse; Fledermaus.

-oust, doused, Faust, joust, oust, soused, spoused; deloused.

-out, bout, clout, doubt, drought, flout, gout, grout, knout, kraut, lout, out, pout, rout, scout, shout, snout, spout, sprout, stout, tout, trout; ablaut, about, devout, lookout, redoubt, throughout, umlaut, without; gadabout, hereabout, knockabout, out-and-out, roundabout, roustabout, sauerkraut, thereabout, waterspout, whereabout.

-outh (-outh), drouth, mouth, south.

-outh (-ōōth). See **-ooth.**

-ove (-ŭv), dove, glove, love, of, shove; above, belove, foxglove, hereof, thereof, unglove, whereof; ladylove, turtledove.

-ove (-ōv), clove, cove, dove, drove, grove, hove, Jove, mauve, rove, shrove, stove, strove, throve, trove, wove; alcove, inwove; borogrove, interwove.

-ove (-ōōv), groove, move, prove, who've, you've; approve, behoove, disprove, improve, remove, reprove; disapprove.

-ow (-ou), bough, bow, brow, chow, cow, dhow, frau, how, now, plough, plow, prow, row, scow, slough, sow, tau, thou, vow, wow; allow, avow, bow-wow, endow, enow, highbrow, hoosegow, kowtow, landau, lowbrow, Mau Mau, meow, Moldau, Moscow, powwow, snowplow, somehow, anyhow, disallow, disavow, middlebrow; Oberammergau.

-ow (-ō), beau, blow, bow, crow, do, doe, dough, eau, Flo, floe, flow; foe, fro, glow, go, grow, hoe, Joe, know, lo, low, mot, mow, no, O, oh, owe, Po, pro, rho, roe, row, sew, show, sloe, slow, snow, so, sow, stow, strow, throe, throw, toe, tow, trow, whoa, woe, Zoe; aglow, ago, although, banjo, below, bestow, Bordeaux, bravo, bubo, bureau, chapeau, château, cocoa, dado, depot, dido, Dido, duo, forego, foreknow, foreshow, Frisco, heigh-ho, hello, jabot,

moonglow, oboe, outgrow, pierrot, poncho,
pou sto, quarto, rainbow, rondeau, Rousseau,
sabot, tableau, tiptoe, toro, trousseau, zero;
abovo, afterglow, albedo, al fresco, allegro,
apropos, buffalo, Buffalo, bungalow, calico,
cameo, Diderot, domino, dos-à-dos. embryo,
Eskimo, falsetto, folio, furbelow, gazebo,
gigolo, Idaho, indigo, memento, Mexico,
mistletoe, mulatto, nuncio, octavo, Ohio,
oleo, overflow, overgrow, overthrow, portico,
portmanteau, potato, proximo, radio,
Romeo, so-and-so, sourdough, stiletto, stu-
dio, tallyho, tobacco, Tokyo, tomato, torero,
torpedo, tremolo, ultimo, undergo, undertow,
vertigo, vireo, volcano; Abednego, Acapulco,
adagio, bravissimo, fortissimo, imbroglio,
incognito, intaglio, magnifico, malapropos,
mustachio, Ontario, pistachio, seraglio; ab
initio, archipelago, banderillero, braggadoc-
cio, duodecimo, impressario, oratorio, pia-
nissimo; generalissimo.

-owd. See **-oud.**

-owed (-ōd). See **-ode.**

-owed (-oud). See **-oud.**

-ower. See **-our.**

-owl, cowl, foul, fowl, growl, howl, jowl, owl,
prowl, scowl, yowl; befoul, waterfowl.

-own (-oun), brown, clown, crown, down,
drown, frown, gown, noun, town; adown,
downtown, embrown, nightgown, pronoun,
renown, uptown; eiderdown, hand-me-down,
tumble-down, upside down.

-own (-ōn). See **-one.**

-owned. See **-ound.**

-ows (-ōz). See **-ose.**

-ows (-ouz). See **-owse.**

-owse, blowse, browse, dowze, drowse, house, rouse, spouse; arouse, carouse, espouse.

　　Also: **-ow** + **-s** (as in *cows*, etc.)

-owth. See **-oth.**

-ox, box, cox, fox, lox, ox, phlox, pox, sox, vox; bandbox, hatbox, icebox, mailbox, postbox, smallpox; chickenpox, equinox, orthodox, paradox; heterodox.

　　Also: **-ock** + **-s** (as in *knocks*, etc.)

-oy, boy, buoy, cloy, coy, goy, joy, oy, ploy, poi, soy, toy, troy, Troy; ahoy, alloy, annoy, convoy, decoy, deploy, destroy, employ, enjoy, envoy, Leroy, Savoy, sepoy, viceroy; corduroy, hoi polloi, Illinois, Iroquois, misemploy, overjoy; hobbledehoy.

-oyed. See **-oid.**

-oys. See **-oise.**

-oze. See **-ose.**

-ub, bub, chub, club, cub, drub, dub, grub, hub, nub, pub, rub, scrub, shrub, snub, stub, sub, tub; hubbub; rub-a-dub, sillabub; Beelzebub.

-ube, boob, cube, rube, Rube, tube; jujube.

-uce. See **-oose.**

-uced. See **-oost.**

-uch. See **-utch.**

-uck, buck, chuck, cluck, duck, luck, muck, pluck, puck, Puck, ruck, shuck, struck, stuck, suck, truck, tuck; amok, amuck, Canuck, potluck, roebuck, woodchuck; horrorstruck, terrorstruck, thunderstruck, wonderstruck.

-ucked. See **-uct.**

-ucks. See **-ux.**

-uct, duct; abduct, conduct, construct. deduct, induct, instruct, obstruct; aqueduct, misconduct, oviduct, usufruct, viaduct.

Also: **-uck** + **-ed** (as in *tucked*, etc.)

-ud, blood, bud, cud, dud, flood, mud, scud, spud, stud, sud, thud; bestud, lifeblood, rosebud.

-ude, brood, crude, dude, feud, food, Jude, lewd, mood, nude, prude, rood, rude, shrewd, snood, you'd, who'd; allude, collude, conclude, delude, denude, elude, étude, exclude, extrude, exude, include, intrude, obtrude, occlude, preclude, prelude, protrude, seclude; altitude, amplitude, aptitude, certitude, desuetude, fortitude, gratitude, habitude, interlude, lassitude, latitude, longitude, magnitude, multitude, platitude, plenitude, promptitude, pulchritude, quietude, rectitude, servitude, solitude, turpitude; beatitude, exactitude, necessitude, similitude, solicitude, vicissitude.

Also: **-ew** + **-ed** (as in *brewed*, etc.)
Also: **-oo** + **-ed** (as in *wooed*, etc.)
Also: **-ue** + **-ed** (as in *pursued*, etc.)

-udge, budge, drudge, fudge, grudge, judge, nudge, sludge, smudge, trudge; adjudge, begrudge, forejudge, misjudge, prejudge.

-ue. See **-ew.**

-ues. See **-ooze** and **-use.**

-uff, bluff, buff, chough, clough, cuff, duff, fluff, gruff, guff, huff, luff, muff, puff, rough, ruff, scruff, scuff, slough, snuff, sough, stuff, tough, tuff; breadstuff, enough, Macduff, rebuff; overstuff, powderpuff.

-ug, bug, chug, drug, dug, hug, jug, lug, mug, plug, pug, rug, shrug, slug, smug, snug, thug, tug; humbug; bunnyhug, doodlebug, jitterbug.

-uge, huge, Scrooge, stooge; refuge; centrifuge, febrifuge, subterfuge, vermifuge.

-uice. See **-oose.**

-uise. See **-ize.**

-uke, duke, fluke, Juke, Luke, puke, snook, spook, uke; archduke, caoutchouc, peruke, rebuke; Heptateuch, Mameluke, Marmaduke, Pentateuch.

-ul (-ŭl), cull, dull, gull, hull, lull, mull, null, scull, skull, trull; annul, mogul, numskull, seagull; disannul.

-ul (-ōōl), bull, full, pull, wool; cupful graceful, lambswool; beautiful, bountiful, dutiful, fanciful, masterful, merciful, pitiful, plentiful, powerful, Sitting Bull, sorrowful, teaspoonful, wonderful, worshipful; tablespoonful.

-ulch, gulch, mulch.

-ule, fuel, mewl, mule, pule, you'll, yule; ampule; molecule, reticule, ridicule, vestibule. See also **-ool.**

-ulge, bulge; divulge, effulge, indulge, promulge.

-ulk, bulk, hulk, skulk, sulk.

-ull. See **-ul.**

-ulp, gulp, pulp, sculp.

-ulse, pulse; appulse, convulse, expulse, impulse, repulse.

-ult, cult; adult, consult, exult, insult, occult, result, tumult; catapult, difficult.

-um, bum, chum, come, crumb, drum, dumb, glum, grum, gum, hum, mum, numb, plum, plumb, rum, scum, slum, some, strum, stum, sum, swum, thrum, thumb; become, benumb, humdrum, spectrum, succumb; burdensome, Christendom, cranium, cumbersome, frolicsome, heathendom, humorsome, kettledrum, laudanum, martyrdom, maximum, medium, mettlesome, minimum, modicum, odium, opium, optimum, overcome, pabulum, pendulum, platinum, premium, quarrelsome, quietsome, radium, speculum, stumble bum, sugar plum, tedium, troublesome, tympanum, vacuum, venturesome, wearisome; adventuresome, aluminum, aquarium, chrysanthemum, compendium, continuum, curriculum, delirium, effluvium, emporium, encomium, exordium, fee-fi-fo-fum, geranium, gymnasium, harmonium, magnesium, millennium, opprobrium, palladium, petroleum, residuum, symposium; auditorium, crematorium, equilibrium, pandemonium, sanitarium.

-umb. See -um.

-ume. See -oom.

-ump, bump, chump, clump, dump, drump, grump, Gump, hump, jump, lump, mump, plump, pump, rump, slump, stump, thump, trump, ump; mugwump.

-un, bun, done, dun, fun, gun, Hun, none, nun, one, pun, run, shun, son, spun, stun, sun, ton, tun, won; begun, homespun, outrun, rerun, someone, undone; Albion, anyone, Chesterton, cinnamon, everyone, galleon, Galveston, garrison, halcyon, orison, overdone, overrun, simpleton, singleton, skeleton, unison, venison; accordion, comparison, oblivion, phenomenon.

-unce, dunce, once.

    Also: **-unt** + **-s** (as in *bunts*, etc.)

-unch, brunch, bunch, crunch, hunch, lunch, munch, punch, scrunch.

-unct, adjunct, defunct, disjunct.

    Also: **-unk** + **-ed** (as in *bunked*, etc.)

-und, bund, fund; fecund, jocund, obtund, refund, rotund; cummerbund, moribund, orotund, rubicund.

    Also: **-un** + **-ed** (as in *stunned*, etc.)

-une. See **-oon.**

-uned. See **-ound.**

-ung, bung, clung, dung, flung, hung, lung, rung, slung, sprung, strung, stung, sung, swung, tongue, wrung, young; among, high-strung, Shantung, unstrung, unsung; Niebe-lung, overhung, underslung.

-unge, lunge, plunge, sponge; expunge; muskel-lunge.

-unk, bunk, chunk, drunk, dunk, flunk, funk, hunk, junk, monk, plunk, punk, shrunk, skunk, slunk, spunk, sunk, trunk; adunc, kerplunk, quidnunc, spelunk.

-unked. See **-unct.**

-unned. See **-und.**

-unt, blunt, brunt, bunt, front, grunt, hunt, punt, runt, shunt, stunt; affront, confront, forefront.

-unts. See **-unce.**

-up, cup, pup, sup, tup, up; hiccup, makeup, setup, teacup, tossup; buttercup.

-upe. See **-oop.**

-upt, abrupt, corrupt, disrupt, erupt; interrupt.
  Also: **-up** + **-ed** (as in *supped*, etc.)

-ur. See **-er.**

-urb. See **-erb.**

-urch, birch, church, lurch, perch, search, smirch; besmirch, research.

-urd, bird, curd, gird, heard, herd, Kurd, surd, third, word; absurd, blackbird, lovebird, songbird, ungird, unheard; hummingbird, ladybird, mockingbird, overheard.
  Also: **-er** + **-ed** (as in *conferred*, etc.)
  Also: **-ir** + **-ed** (as in *stirred*, etc.)
  Also: **-ur** + **-ed** (as in *occurred*, etc.)

-ure, cure, lure, pure, your, you're; allure, cocksure, coiffure, demure, endure, immure, impure, inure, manure, mature, obscure, ordure, procure, secure; amateur, aperture, armature, epicure, forfeiture, furniture, immature, insecure, ligature, overture, portraiture, premature, signature, sinecure; caricature, expenditure, investiture, literature, miniature, temperature; primogeniture. See also **-oor.**

-ures. See **-ours.**

-urf, scurf, serf, surf, turf.

-urge. See **-erge.**

-urk, burke, clerk, dirk, irk, jerk, kirk, lurk, murk, perk, quirk, shirk, smirk, Turk, work; Dunkirk, rework; handiwork, masterwork, overwork, underwork.

-url, Beryl, burl, churl, curl, earl, furl, girl, hurl, knurl, pearl, purl, swirl, twirl, whirl, whorl; uncurl, unfurl.

-urled. See **-orld.**

-urn, Berne, burn, churn, earn, erne, fern, hern, kern, learn, quern, spurn, stern, tern, turn, urn, yearn; adjourn, astern, concern, discern, eterne, intern, Lucerne, return, sojourn, unlearn; overturn, taciturn, unconcern.

-urp, burp, chirp, twerp; usurp.

-urred. See **-urd.**

-urse. See **-erse.**

-ursed. See **-urst.**

-urst, burst, curst, durst, erst, first, Hearst, thirst, verst, worst; accurst, athirst, knack-wurst, outburst, sunburst; liverwurst.
   Also: **-erce** + **-ed** (as in *coerced*, etc.)
   Also: **-erse** + **-ed** (as in *dispersed*, etc.)
   Also: **-urse** + **-ed** (as in *nursed*, etc.)

-urve. See **-erve.**

-us, bus, buss, cuss, fuss, Gus, Hus, muss, plus, pus, Russ, thus, truss, us; cirrus, discuss, nimbus, nonplus, percuss, Remus, stratus; abacus, Angelus, animus, blunderbuss, cumulus, exodus, Hesperus, impetus, incubus, nautilus, octopus, omnibus, Pegasus, platypus, radius, Romulus, Sirius, stimulus, succubus, Tantalus, terminus; esophagus, Leviticus, sarcophagus.
   Also: numerous words ending in **-ous** (as *mutinous, perilous*, etc.)

-use (-ūz), blues, fuse, fuze, mews, muse, news, use; abuse, accuse, amuse, bemuse, confuse, diffuse, disuse, enthuse, excuse, infuse, misuse, refuse, suffuse, transfuse; disabuse, Syracuse.
   See also **-ooze.**
   Also: **-ew** + **-s** (as in *stews*, etc.)

Also: -ue + -s (as in *cues*, etc.)

-use (-o͞os) or (-ūs). See **-oose.**

-use (-o͞oz). See **-ooze.**

-ush (-ŭsh), blush, brush, crush, flush, gush, hush, lush, mush, plush, rush, shush, slush, thrush, tush; hairbrush; underbrush.

-ush (-o͞osh), bush, push, shush, swoosh; ambush; bramblebush, Hindu Kush.

-usk, brusque, busk, dusk, husk, musk, rusk, tusk, Usk.

-uss. See **-us.**

-ussed. See **-ust.**

-ust, bust, crust, dost, dust, gust, just, lust, must, rust, thrust, trust; adjust, adust, august, August, combust, disgust, distrust, encrust, entrust, incrust, mistrust, piecrust, robust, stardust, unjust.

Also: -uss + -ed (as in *fussed*, etc.)

-ut (-ŭt), but, butt, cut, glut, gut, hut, jut, mutt, nut, putt, rut, shut, slut, smut, strut, tut; abut, beechnut, catgut, chestnut, clearcut, crewcut, peanut, rebut, uncut, walnut; betelnut, coconut, halibut, hazelnut, occiput, scuttlebutt.

-ut (-o͞ot) See **-oot.**

-utch, clutch, crutch, Dutch, hutch, much, smutch, such, touch; retouch; inasmuch, insomuch.

-ute, beaut, butte, cute, lute, mute, newt, suit, Ute; acute, astute, Canute, commute, compute, confute, depute, dilute, dispute, hirsute, impute, minute, Piute, pollute, pursuit, refute, repute, salute, transmute, volute; absolute, Aleut, attribute, constitute, destitute, disrepute, dissolute, execute, institute, persecute, prosecute, prostitute, resolute, substitute; electrocute, irresolute, reconstitute. See also -oot.

-uth. See **-ooth.**

-ux, crux, flux, lux, shucks, tux; conflux, efflux, influx.

Also: **-uck** + **-s** (as in *plucks*, etc.)

-uzz, buzz, coz, does, fuzz.

-y, ay, aye, buy, by, bye, cry, die, dry, dye, eye, fie, fly, fry, guy, Guy, hi, hie, high, i, lie, lye, my, nigh, phi, pi, pie, ply, pry, psi, rye, shy, sigh, Skye, sly, spry, spy, sty, Thai, thigh, thy, tie, try, vie, why, wry; ally, apply, awry, belie, comply, decry, defy, deny, descry, espy, goodbye, hereby, imply, July, magpie, mudpie, outcry, outvie, popeye, rely, reply, Shanghai, shoofly, standby, supply, thereby, untie, whereby; abaci, alibi, alkali, alumni, amplify, beautify, butterfly, by-and-by, certify, clarify, classify, codify, crucify, deify, dignify, edify, falsify, fortify, glorify, gratify, horrify, hushaby, justify, lazuli, Lorelei, lullaby, magnify, modify, mollify, mortify, multiply, mystify, notify, nullify, occupy, ossify, pacify, petrify, prophesy, purify, putrefy, qualify, ratify, rectify, sanctify, satisfy, scarify, signify, simplify, specify, stultify, stupefy, terrify, testify, typify, umble-pie, unify, verify, versify, vilify; beatify, disqualify, diversify, exemplify, identify, indemnify, intensify, Lotophagi, personify, preoccupy, solidify; Aegospotami, anthropophagi.

-yle. See -ile.
-yled. See -ild.
-yme. See -ime.
-ymn. See -im.
-ymph, lymph, nymph.
-yne. See -ine.
-ynx. See -inx.
-yp. See -ip.
-ype. See -ipe.
-yph. See -iff.
-ypse. See -ipse.
-yre. See -ire.
-yrrh. See -er.
-ysm. See -ism.
-yst. See -ist.
-yte. See -ite.
-yth. See -ith.
-yve. See -ive.
-yx. See -ix.

Two-Syllable Rhymes

-abard. See **-abbard.**

-abbard, jabbered, scabbard, slabbered, tabard.

-abber (-ă-), blabber, dabber, drabber, grabber, jabber, nabber, slabber, stabber; beslabber.

-abber (-ŏ-). See **-obber.**

-abbered. See **-abbard.**

-abbet. See **-abit.**

-abbey. See **-abby.**

-abbit. See **-abit.**

-abble, babble, dabble, drabble, gabble, grabble, rabble, scabble, scrabble; bedabble, bedrabble.

-abby, abbey, cabby, crabby, flabby, grabby, scabby, shabby, tabby.

-abel. See **-able.**

-aber. See **-abor.**

-abies, babies, rabies, scabies.

-abit, abbot, babbitt, Babbitt, habit, rabbet, rabbit; cohabit, inhabit.

-able, Abel, able, babel, cable, fable, gable label, Mabel, sable, stable, table; disable, enable, unable, unstable.

-abor, caber, labor, neighbor, saber, tabor, Weber; belabor.

-abra, candelabra; abracadabra.

-aby, baby, gaby, maybe.

-accy. See **-acky.**

-acement. See **-asement.**

-acence. See **-ascence.**

-acent, jacent, naissant, nascent; adjacent complacent, complaisant, connascent, renais-

sant, renascent, subjacent; circumjacent,
interjacent.

-aceous. See -acious.

-acet. See -asset.

-achment. See -atchment.

-achne. See -acne.

-acial, facial, glacial, racial, spatial; abbatial,
palatial, prelatial.

-acic. See -assic.

-acile. See -astle.

-acious, gracious, spacious; audacious, bulba-
ceous, cactaceous, capacious, cetaceous,
cretaceous, crustaceous, edacious, fabaceous,
fallacious, feracious, flirtatious, fugacious,
fumacious, fungaceous, gemmaceous, herba-
ceous, Horatius, Ignatius, lappaceous, larda-
ceous, loquacious, marlaceous, mendacious,
micaceous, minacious, misgracious, morda-
cious, palacious, palmaceous, pomaceous,
predaceous, procacious, pugnacious, rampa-
cious, rapacious, rutaceous, sagacious, sala-
cious, sebaceous, sequacious, setaceous,
tenacious, testaceous, tophaceous, ungra-
cious, veracious, vexatious, vinaceous, viva-
cious, voracious; acanaceous, acanthaceous-
alliaceous, amylaceous, arenaceous, campho
raceous, capillaceous, carbonaceous, contu-
macious, corallaceous, coriaceous, disputa-
tious, efficacious, erinaceous, execrations,
farinaceous, ferulaceous, foliaceous, incapa-
cious, liliaceous, olivaceous, orchidaceous,
ostentatious, perspicacious, pertinacious,
resinaceous, saponaceous, violaceous; inef-
ficacious.

-acid, acid, placid.

-acis. See **-asis.**

-acit. See **-asset.**

-acken, blacken, bracken, slacken.

-acker, backer, clacker, cracker, lacquer, packer, slacker; hijacker.

-acket, bracket, flacket, jacket, packet, placket, racket, tacket.

-ackey. See **-acky.**

-ackguard. See **-aggard.**

-ackie. See **-acky.**

-ackish, blackish, brackish, knackish, quackish.

-ackle, cackle, crackle, hackle, macle, quackle, shackle, tackle; debacle, ramshackle, unshackle; tabernacle.

-ackney. See **-acne.**

-ackpot, crackpot, jackpot.

-ackson. See **-axen.**

-acky, 'baccy, Jackie, khaki, knacky, lackey, Saki, tacky, wacky; Nagasaki.

-acle. See **-ackle.**

-acne, acne, hackney; Arachne.

-acon, bacon, Macon.

-acquer. See **-acker.**

-acre. See **-aker.**

-acter. See **-actor.**

-actic, lactic, tactic; didactic, emphractic, galactic, protactic, stalactic, syntactic; parallactic, prophylactic.

-actice, cactus, factice, practice.

-actile, dactyl, tactile, tractile; attractile, contractile, protractile, retractile; pterodactyl.

-action, action, faction, fraction, paction, taction, traction; abstraction, attraction, coaction, compaction, contaction, contraction, detraction, distraction, exaction, extraction, inaction, infraction, protraction, reaction, redaction, refraction, retraction, subaction, subtraction, transaction; arefaction, benefaction, calefaction, counteraction, interaction, labefaction, liquefaction, lubrifaction, malefaction, petrifaction, putrefaction, rarefaction, retroaction, rubefaction, satisfaction, stupefaction, tabefaction, tepefaction, tumefaction; dissatisfaction.

-active, active, tractive; abstractive, attractive, coactive. contractive, detractive, distractive, enactive, inactive, olfactive, protractive, refractive, retractive, subtractive; calefactive, counteractive, petrifactive, putrefactive, retroactive, satisfactive, stupefactive; radioactive.

-actly, abstractly, compactly, exactly; matter-of-factly.

-actor, actor, factor, tractor; abstracter, attracter, climacter, compacter, contractor, detractor, distracter, enacter, exacter, extracter, infractor, olfactor, phylacter, protractor, refractor, retractor, subtracter, transactor; benefactor, malefactor.

-actress, actress, factress; contractress, detractress; benefactress, malefactress.

-acture, facture, fracture; compacture; manufacture.

-actus. See -actice.

-actyl. See -actile.

-acy, Casey, lacy, Macy, racy, précis.

-ada, Dada; armada, cicada, Grenada, haggadah, Nevada.

-adam, Adam, madam; macadam.

-adden, gladden, madden, sadden; engladden.

-adder, adder, bladder, gadder, gladder, ladder, madder, padder, sadder; stepladder.

-addie. See **-addy.**

-adding. See **-odding.**

-addish, baddish, caddish, faddish, maddish, radish, saddish.

-addle (-ă-), addle, daddle, faddle, paddle, raddle, saddle, staddle, straddle; astraddle, skedaddle, unsaddle; fiddle-faddle.

-addle (-ŏ-). See **-oddle.**

-addock, haddock, paddock, raddock, shaddock.

-addy, caddy, daddy, faddy, haddie, laddie, paddy; finnan-haddie, sugar daddy.

-aden, Aden, Haydn, laden, maiden.

-ader, aider, grader, raider, trader; crusader, evader, invader, persuader.

-adger, badger, cadger.

-adi. See **-ady.**

-adic, nomadic, sporadic.

-adiant, gradient, radiant.

-adie. See **-ady.**

-adient. See **-adiant.**

-adish. See **-addish.**

-adle, cradle, ladle; encradle.

-adly, badly, gladly, madly, sadly.

-adness, badness, gladness, madness, sadness.

-ado (-ā dō), dado; crusado, gambado, grenado, scalado, stoccado, tornado; ambuscado, barricado, bastinado, camisado, carbonado, desperado, muscovado, renegado.

-ado (-ä dō), bravado, Mikado, passado, strappado, travado; avocado, Colorado, desperado, El Dorado, imbrocado.

-ady, braidy, cadi, glady, lady, Sadie, shady; belady, cascady, landlady.

-afer, chafer, safer, wafer; cockchafer.

-affer, chaffer, gaffer, kaffir, laugher, zaffer.

-affic. See -aphic.

-affick. See -aphic.

-affir. See -affer.

-affle, baffle, gaffle, haffle, raffle, scraffle, snaffle, yaffle.

-affled, baffled, raffled, scaffold, snaffled.

-affold. See -affled.

-affy, baffy, chaffy, daffy, draffy, taffy.

-after, after, dafter, drafter, grafter, hafter, laughter, rafter, wafter; hereafter, ingrafter, thereafter; hereinafter.

-afty, crafty, drafty, grafty.

-agar. See -agger.

-agate. See -aggot.

-agement, assuagement, encagement, engagement, enragement, presagement.

-ageous, ambagious, contagious, courageous, oragious, outrageous, rampageous, umbrageous; advantageous; disadvantageous.

-ager, cager, gauger, major, pager, sager, stager; assuager, presager.

-aggard, blackguard, haggard, laggard, staggard, staggered, swaggered.

-agger, bragger, dagger, flagger, gagger, jagger, lagger, nagger, ragger, tagger, wagger; one-bagger, three-bagger, two-bagger; agar-agar, carpet-bagger.

-aggered. See **-aggard.**

-aggie. See **-aggy.**

-aggish, haggish, naggish, waggish.

-aggle, daggle, draggle, gaggle, haggle, raggle, straggle, waggle; bedaggle, bedraggle; raggle-taggle.

-aggot, agate, faggot, maggot.

-aggy, Aggie, baggy, craggy, faggy, Maggie, naggy, scraggy, shaggy, slaggy, snaggy, waggy.

-agic, magic, tragic; ellagic, pelagic; archipelagic.

-agile, agile, fragile.

-agious. See **-ageous.**

-agnate, magnate, magnet.

-agnet. See **-agnate.**

-ago (-ā gō), dago, sago; farrago, imago, lumbago, plumbago, virago, vorago.

-ago (-ä gō), Chicago, farrago; Santiago.

-agon, dragon, flagon, wagon; pendragon, snapdragon.

-agrant, flagrant, fragrant, vagrant; infragrant.

-aic, laic; Alcaic, altaic, archaic, deltaic, Hebraic, Judaic, mosaic, Mosaic, Passaic, prosaic, sodaic, spondaic, stanzaic, trochaic, voltaic; algebraic, Alhambraic, pharisaic, Ptolemaic, tesseraic; paradisaic.

-aiden. See **-aden.**

-aider. See **-ader.**

-aidy. See **-ady.**

-aighten. See **-atan.**

-aigner. See **-ainer.**

-ailer, ailer, gaoler, jailer, paler, sailor, squalor, staler, tailor, trailer, whaler.

-ailie. See **-alely.**

-ailiff, bailiff, Caliph.

-ailing, ailing, grayling, paling.

-ailment, ailment, bailment; assailment, bewailment, curtailment, derailment, entailment, impalement, regalement.

-ailor. See **-ailer.**

-aily. See **-alely.**

-aiment. See **-ayment.**

-ainder, attainder, remainder.

-ainer, drainer, gainer, plainer, saner, stainer, strainer, trainer; abstainer, attainer, campaigner, chicaner, complainer, container, profaner, retainer.

-ainful, baneful, gainful, painful; complainful, disdainful.

-ainger. See **-anger.**

-ainly, gainly, mainly, plainly, sanely, vainly humanely, inanely, insanely, mundanely, profanely, ungainly, urbanely.

-ainter, fainter, painter, tainter.

-aintly, faintly, quaintly, saintly; unsaintly.

-ainty, dainty, fainty, feinty.

-ainy, brainy, grainy, rainy, veiny, zany; Eugénie; Allegheny, miscellany.

-airie. See **-ary.**

-airing. See **-aring.**

-airish. See **-arish.**

-airline, airline, hairline.

-airly. See **-arely.**

-airy. See **-ary.**

-aisant. See **-acent.**

-aiser. See -azer.

-aissant. See -acent.

-aisy. See -azy.

-aiter. See -ator.

-aitress. See -atress.

-aiver. See -aver.

-ajor. See -ager.

-ake. See -ocky.

-aker, acre, baker, breaker, faker, fakir, maker, Quaker, raker, shaker, Shaker, taker, waker; bookmaker, dressmaker, grubstaker, heartbreaker, lawbreaker, matchmaker, pacemaker, peacemaker, watchmaker; circuitbreaker, undertaker.

-aki (-ä-). See -acky.

-aki (-ä-). See -ocky.

-akir. See -aker.

-alace. See -allas.

-alad, ballad, salad. See also -alid.

-alan. See -allon.

-alap. See -allop.

-alate. See -allot.

-ale. See -olly.

-alec. See -alic.

-alely, bailie, daily, gaily, grayly, halely, Haley, palely, scaly, shaly, stalely; shillaly; ukelele.

-alement. See -ailment.

-alent, gallant, talent.

-aler. See -ailer.

-alet. See -allot.

-aley. See -alely.

-ali. See -olly.

-alic, Alec, Gallic, malic, phallic, salic; cephalic,

italic, metallic, oxalic, vocalic; brachyce-
phalic; dolichocephalic.

-alice. See -allas.

-alid (-ă-), pallid, valid. See also -alad.

-alid (-ŏ-). See -olid.

-alin. See -allon.

-aling. See -ailing.

-aliph. See -ailiff.

-allad. See -alad.

-allant. See -alent.

-allas, Alice, callous, chalice, Dallas, gallus,
malice, palace, Pallas, phallus.

-allen. See -allon.

-aller. See -allor.

-allet. See -allot.

-allette. See -allot.

-alley. See -ally.

-allic. See -alic.

-allid. See -alid.

-allment, appallment, enthrallment, installment;
disenthrallment.

-allon, Alan, Allen, gallon, Stalin, talon;
ten-gallon.

-allop (-ăl-), gallop, jalap, scallop, shallop;
escallop.

-allop (-ŏl-). See ollop.

-allor, pallor, valor; caballer.

-allot, ballot, mallet, palate, pallet, pallette,
shallot, valet.

-allow (-ăl-), aloe, callow, fallow, hallow,
mallow, sallow, shallow, tallow; marsh-
mallow.

-allow (-ŏl-). See -ollow.

-allus. See -allas.

-ally, alley, bally, challis, dally, galley, pally, rally, sally, Sally, tally, valley; O'Malley; dillydally, shillyshally.

-almest. See **-almist.**

-almist, calmest, palmist, psalmist; embalmist.

-almless, balmless, palmless, psalmless, qualmless.

-almon. See **-ammon.**

-almy. See **-ami.**

-aloe. See **-allow.**

-alon. See **-allon.**

-alor. See **-allor.**

-altar. See **-alter.**

-alter, altar, alter, falter, halter, palter, psalter, salter, vaulter, Walter; assaulter, defaulter, exalter, Gibraltar, unalter.

-alty, faulty, malty, salty, vaulty, walty.

-aly. See **-alely.**

-ama, Brahma, comma, drama, lama, llama, mama, Rama, pajama; cosmorama, Dalai Lama, diorama, Fujiyama, georama, melodrama, neorama, panorama, Yokahama.

-ambeau. See **-ambo.**

-amber, amber, camber, clamber, tambour.

-ambit, ambit, gambit.

-amble, amble, bramble, Campbell, gamble, gambol, ramble, scamble, scramble, shamble; preamble.

-ambo, ambo, crambo, flambeau, Sambo, zambo.

-ambol. See **-amble.**

-ambour. See **-amber.**

-ameful, blameful, flameful, shameful.

-amel, camel, Campbell, mammal, trammel; enamel, entrammel.

-amely, gamely, lamely, namely, tamely.

-ami, balmy, palmy, swami, Tommy; pastrami, salami.

-amin. See **-amine.**

-amine, famine, gamin; examine; cross-examine, reëxamine. See also **-ammon.**

-amish, Amish, famish, rammish; affamish, enfamish.

-amlet, camlet, hamlet, Hamlet, samlet.

-ammal. See **-amel.**

-ammar. See **-ammer.**

-ammel. See **-amel.**

-ammer, clamor, crammer, dammer, gammer, glamour, grammar, hammer, rammer, shammer, slammer, stammer, yammer; enamor, sledge-hammer, windjammer; ninnyhammer, yellowhammer.

-ammish. See **-amish.**

-ammon, Ammon, gammon, mammon, salmon; backgammon. See also **-amine.**

-ammy, chamois, clammy, gammy, hammy, mammy, Sammy, shammy, tammy.

-amois. See **-ammy.**

-amon. See **-ayman.**

-amor. See **-ammer.**

-amos. See **-amous.**

-amour. See **-ammer.**

-amous, Amos, famous, hamous, squamous, shamus; biramous, mandamus; ignoramus; Nostradamus.

-ampas. See **-ampus.**

-ampbell. See **-amble** or **-amel.**

-amper, camper, cramper, damper, hamper, pamper, scamper, stamper, tamper, tramper.

-ample, ample, sample, trample; ensample, example.

-ampler, ampler, sampler, trampler; exampler.

-ampus, campus, grampus, pampas.

-amus. See **-amous.**

-ana, anna, Anna, Hannah, manna; banana, bandanna, Diana, Havana, hosanna, Montana, Nirvana, savannah, Savannah, sultana, Urbana, zenana; Indiana, Juliana, Pollyanna, Susquehanna; Americana, Louisiana.

-anate. See **-anet.**

-anet, gannet, granite, Janet, planet; pomegranate.

-ancer, answer, cancer, chancer, dancer, glancer, lancer, prancer; advancer, enhancer, entrancer, merganser, romancer; chiromancer, gandy-dancer, geomancer, necromancer.

-ancet. See **-ansit.**

-anchion. See **-ansion.**

-anchor. See **-anker.**

-anchored. See **-ankered.**

-ancor. See **-anker.**

-ancy, chancy, Clancy, dancy, fancy, Nancy; mischancy, unchancy; aldermancy, austromancy, belomancy, ceromancy, chiromancy, cleromancy, consonancy, crithomancy, gastromancy, geomancy, gyromancy, hesitancy, hieromancy, hydromancy, lithomancy, mendicancy, militancy, myomancy, necromancy, occupancy, oenomancy, onomancy, pedomancy, petulancy, psychomancy, sciomancy, sibilancy, spodomancy, stichomancy, supplicancy, sycophancy, tephramancy, termagancy; aleuromancy, anthropomancy, axinomancy, bibliomancy, botanomancy, catoptromancy, coscinomancy, crystallomancy, exorbitancy, extravagancy, exuberancy, lecanomancy, ophiomancy, ornithomancy, precipitancy, sideromancy, significancy; alectoromancy, alectryomancy, meteoromancy.

-anda, Amanda, Miranda, veranda; memoranda, propaganda.

-andal. See **-andle.**

-andant, commandant, demandant.

-andem. See **-andom.**

-ander (-ăn-), candor, dander, gander, glander, grander, pander, sander, slander; backhander, bystander, commander, dittander, Leander, meander, Menander, philander, pomander; Alexander, coriander, gerrymander, oleander, salamander.

-ander (-ŏn-). See **-onder.**

-andbi. See **-andy.**

-andi. See **-andy.**

-andid. See **-andied.**

-andied, bandied, brandied, candid, candied; uncandid.

-anding, banding, branding, landing, standing; demanding, disbanding, expanding, outstanding; notwithstanding, understanding.

-andish, blandish, brandish, grandish, Standish; outlandish.

-andit, bandit, pandit.

-andle, candle, dandle, handle, sandal, scandal, vandal; manhandle, mishandle.

-andler, candler, chandler, dandler, handler.

-andom, mandom, random, tandem; avizandum, memorandum.

-andor. See **-ander.**

-andsome. See **-ansom.**

-andstand, bandstand, grandstand, handstand.

-andum. See **-andom.**

-andy, Andy, bandy, brandy, candy, dandy, Gandhi, gandy, handy, Mandy, pandy, randy, sandy, Sandy; unhandy; jaborandi, jackadandy.

-aneful. See **-ainful.**

-anel. See **-annel.**

-anely. See **-ainly.**

-aneous, cutaneous, extraneous, spontaneous; instantaneous, miscellaneous, simultaneous; contemporaneous, extemporaneous.

-aner. See **-ainer.**

-anger (-ăng ər), anger, angor, banger, clangor, ganger, hangar, hanger, languor; har^anguer, straphanger, paper hanger.

-anger (-ān jər), changer, danger, Grainger, granger, manger, ranger, stranger; arranger, bushranger, deranger, endanger, estranger, exchanger; disarranger, interchanger, money changer.

-angle, angle, bangle, brangle, dangle, jangle, mangle, spangle, strangle, tangle, twangle, wangle, wrangle; bemangle, bespangle, embrangle, entangle, quadrangle, triangle, untangle; disentangle, interjangle.

-angled, newfangled, star-spangled.

> so: **-angle** + **-ed** (as in *tangled*, etc.)
> mango, tango; contango, fandango, Pago.

-angor. See -anger.

-anguer. See -anger.

-anguish, anguish, languish.

-anguor. See -anger.

-angy, mangy, rangy.

-anic, panic, tannic; botanic, Brahmanic, Britannic, galvanic, Germanic, mechanic, organic, rhodanic, satanic, sultanic, tetanic, titanic, tyrannic, volcanic, vulcanic; aldermanic, charlatanic, diaphanic, lexiphanic, Messianic, oceanic, Ossianic, Puritanic, talismanic; ferricyanic, hydrocyanic, valerianic; interoceanic.

-anics, annex, panics; humanics, mechanics.

-anil. See -annel.

-anion, banyan, canyon; companion.

-anish, banish, clannish, mannish, planish, Spanish, vanish; evanish.

-anite. See -anet.

-ankard. See -ankered.

-anker, anchor, blanker, canker, clanker, danker, hanker, rancor, ranker, spanker, tanker.

-ankered, anchored, cankered, hankered, tankard.

-ankle, ankle, rankle.

-ankly, blankly, dankly, frankly, lankly, rankly.

-anless, manless, planless.

-anna. See -ana.

-annah. See -ana.

-annal. See -annel.

-annel, anil, annal, cannel, channel, flannel, panel, scrannel; empanel.

-**anner**, banner, canner, manner, manor, planner, scanner, spanner, tanner.

-**annet.** See -**anet.**

-**annex.** See -**anics.**

-**annic.** See -**anic.**

-**annie.** See -**anny.**

-**annish.** See -**anish.**

-**annual.** See -**anual.**

-**anny**, Annie, branny, canny, clanny, cranny, Danny, fanny, Fanny, granny, Mannie, nanny; uncanny; hootenanny.

-**anor.** See -**anner.**

-**anser.** See -**ancer.**

-**ansett.** See -**ansit.**

-**ansion**, mansion, panchion, scansion, stanchion; expansion.

-**ansit**, lancet, transit; Narragansett.

-**ansom**, handsome, hansom, ransom, transom; unhandsome.

-**answer.** See -**ancer.**

-**ansy**, pansy, tansy; chimpanzee.

-**anta**, Santa; Atlanta, infanta, Vedanta; Atalanta.

-**antam**, bantam, phantom.

-**ante.** See -**anty.**

-**anteau.** See -**anto.**

-**antel.** See -**antle.**

-**anter**, banter, canter, cantor, chanter, grantor, panter, planter, ranter; decanter, descanter, enchanter, implanter, instanter, Levanter, recanter, transplanter, trochanter.

-**anther**, anther, panther.

-**anti.** See -**anty.**

-**antic**, antic, frantic, mantic; Atlantic, gigantic,

pedantic, romantic; chiromantic, consonantic, corybantic, geomantic, hierophantic, hydromantic, necromantic, pyromantic, sycophantic, transatlantic.

-antine, Byzantine, Levantine; adamantine, elephantine.

-antle, cantle, mantel, mantle, scantle; immantle.

-antler, antler, mantler, pantler; dismantler.

-antling, bantling, mantling, scantling; dismantling.

-anto, canto, panto; coranto, portmanteau; Esperanto, quo warranto.

-antom. See **-antam.**

-antor. See **-anter.**

-antry, chantry, gantry, pantry.

-anty, ante, anti, auntie, chanty, Dante, scanty, shanty; Ashanti, Bacchante, andante, chianti, infante, dilettante.

-anual, annual, manual; Emmanuel.

-anuel. See **-anual.**

-any (-ā-). See **-ainy.**

-any (-ĕ-). See **-enny.**

-anyan. See **-anion.**

-anyon. See **-anion.**

-anza, stanza; bonanza; Sancho Panza; extravaganza.

-anzee. See **-ansy.**

-aoler. See **-ailer.**

-apal. See **-aple.**

-ape. See **-appy.**

-apel. See **-apple.**

-apen, capon; misshapen, unshapen.

-aper, aper, caper, draper, paper, sapor, taper,

tapir, vapor; flypaper, landscape, newspaper, sandpaper, skyscraper.

-aphic, graphic, maffick, traffic; seraphic; autographic, biographic, cacographic, calligraphic, cartographic, chirographic, clinographic, cosmographic, crytographic, diagraphic, epigraphic, epitaphic, ethnographic, geographic, hierographic, holographic, hydrographic, ichnographic, lithographic, logographic, monographic, orthographic, pantographic, paragraphic, pasigraphic, petrographic, phonographic, photographic, polygraphic, pornographic, scenographic, sciagraphic, seismographic, stenographic, stratigraphic, stylographic, telegraphic, topographic, typographic, xylographic; bibliographic, choreographic, heliographic, heterographic, ideographic, lexicographic, physiographic; autobiographic, cinematographic.

-apid, rapid, sapid, vapid.

-apir. See **-aper.**

-apist, papist, rapist; escapist, landscapist.

-aple, maple, papal, staple.

-apless, capless, hapless, napless, sapless, strapless.

-apling. See **-appling.**

-apnel, grapnel, shrapnel.

-apon. See **-apen.**

-apor. See **-aper.**

-apper, capper, clapper, dapper, flapper, mapper, napper, sapper, tapper, trapper, wrapper; entrapper, fly-sapper, kidnaper; handicapper, understrapper, whippersnapper.

-appet, lappet, tappet.

-appie. See **-appy.**

-apple, apple, chapel, dapple, grapple, scapple, scrapple, thrapple; love apple, pineapple.

-appling, dappling, grappling, sapling.

-appy, chappie, flappy, happy, knappy, nappy, sappy, scrappy, snappy; serape, slap-happy, unhappy.

-apter, apter, captor, chapter; adapter, recaptor.

-aptest. See **-aptist.**

-aption, caption; adaption, contraption, recaption.

-aptist, aptest, baptist, raptest; adaptest, inaptest; anabaptist.

-aptor. See **-apter.**

-apture, capture, rapture; enrapture, recapture.

-ara, Clara, Sarah; mascara, tiara.

-arab, arab, Arab, scarab.

-arage. See **-arriage.**

-araoh. See **-arrow.**

-arass. See **-arras.**

-arat. See **-aret.**

-arbel. See **-arble.**

-arber. See **-arbor.**

-arbered. See **-arboard.**

-arble (-är-), barbel, garbel, garble, marble; enmarble.

-arble (-ôr-), corbel, warble.

-arboard, barbered, harbored, larboard, starboard.

-arbor, arbor, barber, harbor; unharbor.

-arbored. See **-arboard.**

-arcel, parcel, sarcel, tarsal; metatarsal.

-archal. See **-arkle.**

-archer, archer, marcher, parcher, starcher; departure.

-archy, barky, darky, larky, marquee, sparky; malarky; heterarchy, hierarchy, matriarchy, oligarchy, patriarchy.

-arden (-är-), Arden, garden, harden, pardon; beer-garden, bombardon, caseharden, enharden.

-arden (-ôr-). See **-ordon.**

-arder (-är-), ardor, carder, harder, larder; bombarder, Cunarder.

-arder (-ôr-). See **-order.**

-ardon. See **-arden.**

-ardor. See **-arder.**

-ardy, hardy, lardy, tardy; foolhardy, Lombardy, Picardy.

-arel. See **-arrel.**

-arely, barely, fairly, rarely, squarely, yarely; unfairly; debonairly.

-arent, arrant, parent; apparent, transparent.

-aret, carat, caret, carrot, claret, garret, karat, parrot.

-arfish, garfish, starfish.

-argent, argent, sergeant.

-arger, charger, larger; enlarger.

-argo, Argo, argot, cargo, largo, Margot; botargo, embargo, Wells Fargo; supercargo.

-argot. See **-argo.**

-ari (-âr-). See **-ary.**

-ari (-är-). See **-arry.**

-arian. See **-arion.**

-aric, baric, carrick, Garrick; agaric, barbaric, Pindaric; Balearic, cinnabaric. See also **-arrack.**

-arid. See **-arried.**

-aried. See **-arried.**

-arier. See **-arrier.**

-aring, airing, daring, fairing; seafaring, tale-bearing, wayfaring; overbearing.

-arion, Arian, Aryan, carrion, clarion, Marian, Marion.

-arious, Darius, various; Aquarius, bifarious, contrarious, gregarious, hilarious, nefarious, ovarious, precarious, vicarious; multifarious, Sagittarius, temerarious.

-aris, Paris, Harris, heiress; Polaris. See also **-arras.**

-arish, barish, bearish, garish, parish, rarish, sparish, squarish; debonairish.

-arius. See **-arious.**

-arken, darken, hearken.

-arkish, darkish, larkish, sparkish.

-arkle, darkle, sparkle; monarchal; patriarchal.

-arkling, darkling, sparkling.

-arkly, darkly, sparkly, starkly.

-arky. See **-archy.**

-arlak. See **-arlic.**

-arlech. See **-arlic.**

-arler, gnarler, marler, parlor, snarler.

-arlet, carlet, harlot, scarlet, starlet, varlet.

-arley. See **-arly.**

-arlic, garlic, Harlech, sarlak; pilgarlic.

-arlie. See **-arly.**

-arling, darling, marling, snarling, sparling, starling.

-arlor. See **-arler.**

-arlot. See **-arlet.**

-arly, barley, Charlie, gnarly, parley, snarly;
  particularly.

-armer, armor, charmer, farmer; snake charmer;
  baby farmer.

-arming, arming.

  Also: **-arm** + **-ing** (as in *charming*, etc.)

-armless, armless, harmless.

-armor. See **-armer.**

-army, army, barmy.

-arnal. See **-arnel.**

-arnel, carnal, charnel, darnel.

-arner, garner, harner.

-arness, farness, harness.

-arning. See **-orning.**

-arnish, garnish, tarnish, varnish.

-aro. See **-arrow.**

-arol. See **-arrel.**

-aron, baron, barren, Charon, marron, Sharon;
  fanfaron.

-arper, harper, sharper.

-arquee. See **-archy.**

-arrack, arrack, barrack, carrack. See also
  -aric.

-arrant. See **-arent.**

-arras, arras, harass; embarrass. See also **-aris.**

-arrel (-ăr-), barrel, carol, Carol, Carroll;
  apparel.

-arrel (-ôr-). See **-oral.**

-arren (-ă-). See **-aron.**

-arren (-ŏ-). See **-oreign.**

-arret. See **-aret.**

-arriage, carriage, marriage; disparage, mis-
  carriage, mismarriage; intermarriage.

-arrick. See **-aric.**

-arrie. See **-ary.**

-arried, arid, carried, harried, married, parried, tarried, varied; miscarried, remarried, unmarried, unvaried; intermarried.

-arrier, barrier, carrier, charier, farrier, harrier, marrier, parrier, tarrier.

-arrion. See **-arion.**

-arris. See **-aris.**

-arron. See **-aron.**

-arrot. See **-aret.**

-arrow, arrow, barrow, faro, farrow, harrow, Harrow, marrow, narrow, Pharaoh, sparrow, taro, yarrow; bolero, dinero, pierrot, primero, sombrero, torero; caballero; banderillero, Embarcadero.

-arry (-är-), barry, charry, sari, scarry, sparry, starry, tarry; aracari, carbonari, charivari, hari-kari, Mata Hari. See also **-orry.**

-arry (-âr-). See **-ary.**

-arsal. See **-arcel.**

-arshal. See **-artial.**

-arsley, parsley, sparsely.

-arson, arson, Carson, parson; mene mene tekel upharsin.

-artan. See **-arten.**

-arte. See **-arty.**

-arten, barton, carton, hearten, marten, martin, Martin, smarten, Spartan, tartan; dishearten, enhearten; kindergarten.

-arter, barter, carter, charter, darter, garter, martyr, starter, tartar; bemartyr, self-starter, upstarter.

-artful, artful, cartful, heartful.

-artial, marshal, Marshall, martial, partial; immartial, impartial.

-artin. See **-arten.**

-artist, artist, Chartist, smartest.

-artle, dartle, startle.

-artlet, heartlet, martlet, partlet, tartlet.

-artly, partly, smartly, tartly.

-artner, heartener, partner, smartener; disheartener.

-arton. See **-arten.**

-artridge, cartridge, partridge.

-arture. See **-archer.**

-arty, arty, hearty, party, smarty; Astarte, ex parte.

-artyr. See **-arter.**

-arval. See **-arvel.**

-arvel, carvel, larval, marvel.

-arvest, carvest, harvest, starvest.

-arving, carving, starving.

-ary, airy, Carrie, carry, chary, dairy, eyrie, fairy, Gary, hairy, harry, Larry, marry, Mary, merry, nary, parry, prairie, scary, tarry, vary, wary; canary, contrary, miscarry, unchary, unwary, vagary; actuary, adversary, ancillary, antiquary, arbitrary, capillary, cassowary, cautionary, centenary, commentary, commissary, corollary, culinary, customary, dictionary, dietary, dignitary, dromedary, estuary, February, formulary, functionary, hari-kari, honorary, intermarry, Janissary, January, legendary, legionary, literary, luminary, mercenary, military, momentary, monetary, mortuary, necessary, ordinary, passionary, planetary, prebendary, pulmonary, reliquary, salivary, salutary, sanctuary, sanguinary, sanitary, scapulary, secondary, secretary, sedentary, seminary, solitary, stationary, statuary, sublunary, sumptuary, temporary, tertiary, Tipperary, titulary, tributary, tumulary, tutelary, visionary, voluntary, vulnerary; ablutionary, accustomary, additionary, adminculary, apothecary, confectionary, constabulary, contemporary, contributary, depositary, epistolary, fiduciary, hereditary, imaginary, incendiary, involuntary, obituary, pecuniary, proprietary, residuary, ubiquitary, vocabulary, voluptuary; accidentiary, beneficiary, evolutionary, extraordinary, intermediary. See also **-erry.**

-aryan. See **-arion.**

-asal, basal, basil, hazel, nasal, phrasal; appraisal, witch hazel.

-ascal, paschal, rascal.

-ascar. See **-asker.**

-ascence, nascence; complacence, obeisance, renascence.

-ascent. See **-acent.**

-asement, basement, casement, placement; abasement, begracement, belacement, debasement, defacement, displacement, effacement, embracement, enlacement, erasement, misplacement, retracement, subbasement; interlacement.

-aser. See **-azer.**

-asey. See **-acy.**

-asian. See **-asion.**

-asher, Dasher, rasher; haberdasher.

Also: **-ash** + **-er** (as in *splasher*, etc.)

-ashion. See **-assion.**

-ashy (-ă-), ashy, flashy, mashie, mashy, plashy, slashy, splashy, trashy.

-ashy (-ŏ-). See **-oshy.**

-asion, Asian, suasion; abrasion, Caucasian, dissuasion, equation, Eurasian, evasion, invasion, occasion, persuasion, pervasion.

-asis, basis, crasis, glacis, phasis; oasis.

-asive, suasive; assuasive, dissuasive, evasive, invasive, persuasive, pervasive.

-asker, asker, basker, lascar, masker; Madagascar.

-asket, basket, casket, flasket, gasket.

-ason. See **-asten.**

-aspar. See **-asper.**

-asper, asper, Caspar, gasper, jasper, Jasper.
  Also: **-asp + -er** (as in *clasper*, etc.)

-assal. See **-astle.**

-assel. See **-astle.**

-asses, molasses.
  Also: **-ass + -es** (as in *classes*, etc.)

-asset, asset, basset, brasset, facet, fascet, placet, tacit.

-assic, classic; boracic, Jurassic, potassic, sebacic, thoracic, Triassic.

-assie. See **-assy.**

-assing, passing.
  Also: **-ass + -ing** (as in *amassing*, etc.)

-assion, ashen, fashion, passion, ration; Circassian, compassion, dispassion, impassion.

-assive, massive, passive; impassive.

-assle. See **-astle.**

-assock, cassock, hassock.

-assy, brassie, brassy, chassis, classy, gassy,

glassy, grassy, lassie, massy, sassy; morassy;
Malagasy, Tallahassee; Haile Selassie.

-astard, bastard, castored, dastard, mastered,
plastered.

-asteful, tasteful, wasteful; distasteful.

-asten, basin, caisson, chasten, hasten, mason.

-aster (-ā-), baster, chaster, haster, paster, taster,
waster.

-aster (-ă-), aster, Astor, blaster, caster, castor,
faster, master, pastor, piaster, plaster, vaster;
bandmaster, beplaster, cadaster, disaster,
schoolmaster, taskmaster; alabaster, burgo-
master, criticaster, medicaster, oleaster, over-
master, poetaster, quartermaster, Zoroaster.

-astered. See **-astard.**

-astic, clastic, drastic, mastic, plastic, spastic;
bombastic, dichastic, dynastic, elastic, em-
plastic, fantastic, gymnastic, monastic, pro-
plastic, sarcastic, scholastic; amphiblastic,
anaclastic, antiphrastic, bioplastic, ceroplas-
tic, chiliastic, Hudibrastic, inelastic, meta-
phrastic, onomastic, orgiastic, paraphrastic,
periphrastic, pleonastic, protoplastic, scholi-
astic; antonomastic, ecclesiastic, encomiastic,
enthusiastic, iconoclastic.

-asting, everlasting.

Also: **-ast** + **-ing** (as in *fasting*, etc.)

-astle, castle, facile, hassle, passel, tassel, vassal,
wassail, wrastle; entassel, envassal.

-astly, ghastly, lastly, vastly.

-astor. See **-aster.**

-astored. See **-astard.**

-asty (-ă-), blasty, nasty, vasty.

-asty (-ā-), hasty, pasty, tasty.

-asy. See -assy.

-ata (-ātə), beta, data, eta, strata, theta, zeta; albata, dentata, errata, pro rata; postulata, ultimata, vertebrata; invertebrata.

-ata (-ätə), data, strata; cantata, errata, regatta, sonata, serenata; inamorata.

-atal, datal, fatal, natal, statal; postnatal; antenatal.

-atan, Satan, straighten, straiten.

-atant. See -atent.

-atcher, catcher, matcher, patcher, scratcher, snatcher, stature, thatcher; dispatcher, detacher, flycatcher.

-atchet, hatchet, latchet, ratchet.

-atchman, Scotchman, watchman.

-atchment, catchment, hatchment, ratchment; attachment, detachment, dispatchment.

-ateau, chateau, plateau; mulatto.

-ateful, fateful, grateful, hateful, plateful.

-atent, blatant, latent, natant, patent.

-ater (-ô-), daughter, slaughter, tauter, water; backwater, firewater, manslaughter, stepdaughter.

-ater (-ā-). See -ator.

-ather (-ătͪr-), blather, gather, lather, rather; foregather.

-ather (-ŏtͪr-). See -other.

-athos, Athos, bathos, pathos.

-atial. See -acial.

-atian. See -ation.

-atic, attic, static; aquatic, astatic, asthmatic, chromatic, Dalmatic, dogmatic, dramatic, ecbatic, ecstatic, emphatic, erratic, fanatic, hepatic, lymphatic, phlegmatic, piratic, pneu-

matic, pragmatic, prismatic, quadratic, rheu-
matic, Socratic, stigmatic, thematic, trau-
matic; achromatic, acrobatic, Adriatic,
aerostatic, aplanatic, aromatic, Asiatic, auto-
cratic, automatic, bureaucratic, democratic,
dichromatic, diplomatic, eleatic, emblematic,
enigmatic, Hanseatic, hieratic, hydrostatic,
mathematic, mobocratic, morganatic, muri-
atic, numismatic, operatic, pancreatic, pluto-
cratic, problematic, symptomatic, systematic;
adiabatic, anagrammatic, aristocratic, axio-
matic, epigrammatic, idiocratic, idiomatic,
melodramatic, physiocratic; idiosyncratic.

-atim, literatim, seriatim, verbatim. See also
-atum.

-atin, matin, Latin, patin, platen, satin; Man-
hattan, Powhattan. See also -atten.

-ation, Haitian, nation, ration, station; ablation,
aeration, Alsatian, carnation, castration,
causation, cessation, citation, collation, cre-
ation, cremation, Dalmatian, damnation,
deflation, dictation, dilation, donation, dura-
tion, elation, equation, filtration, fixation,
flirtation, flotation, formation, foundation,
frustration, gestation, gradation, gyration,
hortation, inflation, lactation, laudation,
lavation, legation, libation, location, migra-
tion, mutation, narration, natation, negation,
notation, nugation, oblation, oration, ova-
tion, phonation, plantation, predation, priva-
tion, probation, prostration, pulsation,
quotation, relation, rogation, rotation,
sensation, serration, stagnation, taxation,
temptation, translation, vacation, venation,

vexation, vibration, vocation; abdication, aberration, abjuration, ablactation, abnegation, abrogation, acceptation, acclamation, accusation, actuation, adaptation, adjuration, admiration, adoration, adulation, adumbration, aerostation, affectation, affirmation, aggravation, aggregation, agitation, allegation, allocation, alteration, altercation, alternation, angulation, amputation, animation, annexation, annotation, appellation, application, approbation, arbitration, arrogation, aspiration, assignation, association, attestation, augmentation, auscultation, aviation, avocation, bifurcation, botheration, calcination, calculation, cancellation, captivation, castigation, celebration, circulation, cogitation, collocation, coloration, combination, commendation, commutation, compensation, compilation, complication, computation, concentration, condemnation, condensation, confirmation, confiscation, conflagration, conformation, confrontation, confutation, congelation, congregation, conjugation, conjuration, connotation, consecration, conservation, consolation, constellation, consternation, consultation, consummation, contamination, contemplation, conversation, convocation, copulation, coronation, corporation, correlation, corrugation, coruscation, culmination, cultivation, cumulation, debarkation, decimation, declamation, declaration, declination, decoration, decussation, dedication, defalcation, defamation, defecation, defloration, deformation, degradation, delectation, delegation, demonstration, denotation, denudation, depilation, deportation, depravation, deprecation, depredation, deprivation, deputation, derivation, derogation, desecration, desiccation, designation, desolation, desperation, destination, detestation, detonation, devastation, deviation, dislocation, dispensation, disputation, dissertation, dissipation, distillation. divagation, divination, domination, duplication, education, elevation, elongation, emanation, emendation, emigration, emulation, enervation, equitation, eructation, estimation, estivation, evocation, exaltation, excavation, excitation, exclamation, execration, exhalation, exhortation, expectation, expiation, expiration, explanation, explication, exploitation, exploration, exportation, expurgation, extirpation, extrication, exudation, exultation, fabrication, fascination, federation, fenestration, fermentation, flagellation, fluctuation, fomentation, fornication, fulmination, fumigation, generation, germination, graduation, granulation, gravitation, habitation, hesitation, hibernation, ideation, illustration, imitation, implantation, implication, importation, imprecation, impregnation, incantation, incitation, inclination, incubation, inculcation, indentation, indication, indignation, infestation, infiltration, inflammation, information, inhalation, innovation, inspiration, installation, instigation, instillation, intimation, intonation, inundation, invitation, invocation, irrigation, irritation, isolation, jubilation, laceration, lamentation, lamination, legislation, levigation, levitation, liberation, limitation, litigation, lubrication, lucubration, maceration, machination, malformation, mastication, maturation, mediation, medication, meditation, mensuration, ministration, mitigation, moderation, modulation, molestation, mutilation, navigation, numeration, obfuscation, objurgation, obligation, obscuration, observation, obviation, occupation, operation, ordination, orchestration, oscillation, osculation, palpitation, penetration, percolation, perforation, permeation, permutation, peroration, perpetration, perspiration, perturbation, population, postulation, predication, preparation, presentation, preservation, proclamation, procreation, procuration, profanation, profligation, prolongation, protestation, provocation, publication, punctuation, radiation, recantation, recitation, reclamation, recreation, reformation, refutation, registration, regulation, relaxation, remonstration, renovation, reparation, reputation, reservation, resignation, respiration, restoration, retardation, revelation, revocation, ruination, rumination, rustication, salutation, scintillation, segmentation, segregation, separation, sequestration, sibilation, simulation, situation, speculation, spoliation, sternutation, stimulation, sublimation, subornation, suffocation, supplication, suppuration, suspiration, syncopation, termination, titillation, toleration, transformation, transplantation, transportation, trepidation, tribulation, triplication, usurpation, vaccination, vacillation, valuation, variation, vegetation, veneration, ventilation, vindication, violation, visitation, vitiation; abbreviation, abomination, acceleration, accentuation, accommodation, accreditation, accumulation, adjudication, administration, adulteration, affiliation, agglutination, alienation, alleviation, alliteration, amalgamation, amplification, annihilation, annunciation, anticipation, appreciation, appropriation, approximation, argumentation, articulation, asphyxiation, assassination, assimilation, attenuation, authorization, brutalization, calcification, calumniation, canonization, capitulation, carbonization, catechization, circumvallation, clarification, coagulation, codification, cohabitation, columniation, commemoration, commensuration, commiseration, communication, concatenation, conciliation, confederation, configuration, conglomeration, congratulation, consideration, consolidation, continuation, cooperation, coordination, corroboration, crystallization, debilitation, degeneration, deification, deliberation, delimitation, delineation, denomination, denunciation, depopulation, depreciation, despoliation, determination, dignification, dilapidation, disapprobation, discoloration, discrimination, disfiguration, disinclination, disintegration, dissemination, disseveration, dissimulation, dissociation, documentation, domestication, edification, effectuation, ejaculation, elaboration, elimination, elucidation, emaciation, emancipation, emasculation, embarkation, enumeration, enunciation, equalization, equilibration, equivocation, eradication, evacuation, evaporation, evisceration, exacerbation, exaggeration, examination, exasperation, excoriation, exhilaration, exoneration, expatiation, expectoration, expostulation, expropriation, extenuation, extermination, facilitation, falsification, felicitation, fertilization, fortification, fossilization, galvanization, gesticulation, glorification, gratification, habilitation, habituation, hallucination, harmonization, Hellenization, horrification, humiliation, hypothecation, idealization, illumination, imagination, immoderation, inauguration, incarceration, incineration, incorporation, incrimination, inebriation, infatuation, initiation, inoculation, insemination, insinuation, interpolation, interpretation, interrogation, intoxication, investigation, irradiation, justification, legalization, legitimation, manifestation, manipulation, matriculation, melioration, misinformation, modernization, modification, mollification, moralization, mortification, multiplication, mystification, nasalization, negotiation, notification, obliteration, origination, organization, ossification, pacification, participation, perambulation, peregrination, perpetuation, precipitation, predestination, predomination, premeditation, preoccupation, prevarication, procrastination, prognostication, pronunciation, propitiation, protuberation, purification, qualification, ramification, ratification, realization, reciprocation, recommendation, recrimination, rectification, recuperation, refrigeration, regeneration, regurgitation, reiteration, rejuvenation, remuneration, renunciation, representation, repudiation, resuscitation, retaliation, reverberation, sanctification, scarification, signification, solemnization, sophistication, specialization, specification, subordination, symbolization, variegation, versification, vituperation, vivification, vociferation; amelioration, beatification, circumnavigation, contraindication, cross-examination, demonetization, deterioration, differentiation, discontinuation, disqualification, diversification, electrification, excommunication, exemplification, experimentation, extemporization, identification, inconsideration, indemnification, individuation, misrepresentation, naturalization, personification, predetermination, ratiocination, recapitulation, reconciliation, spiritualization, superannuation, supererogation, tintinnabulation, transubstantiation.

-atius. See **-acious.**

-ative, dative, native, sative, stative; creative, dilative; aggregative, cogitative, cumulative, designative, emulative, estimative, generative, hesitative, imitative, innovative, legislative, meditative, operative, predicative, procreative, quantitative, radiative, speculative, terminative, vegetative, violative; appreciative, associative, communicative, continuative, corroborative.

-atless, Atlas, hatless.

-atling. See **-attling.**

-atly, flatly, patly, rattly.

-ato (-ā-), Cato, Plato; potato, tomato.

-ato (-ä-), château; legato, mulatto, tomato. staccato; obbligato, pizzicato; inamorato. See also **-otto.**

-ator, cater, crater, freighter, gaiter, greater, later. mater, pater, traitor, waiter; creator, cunctator, curator, dictator, dumbwaiter, equator, first-rater, scrutator, spectator. testator, third-rater; alligator, alma mater, carburetor, commentator, conservator, second-rater.

    Also: **-ate** + **-er** or **-or** (as in *hater*, *cultivator*, etc.)

-atress, traitress, waitress; creatress, dictatress, spectatress; imitatress.

-atrix, matrix; cicatrix, spectatrix, testatrix; aviatrix, generatrix, mediatrix; administratrix.

-atron, matron, natron, patron.

-atten, baton, batten, fatten, flatten, paten, platen. ratten. See also **-atin.**

-atter (-ă-), attar, batter, blatter, chatter, clatter, fatter, flatter, hatter, latter, matter, patter, ratter, satyr, scatter, shatter, smatter, spatter, splatter, tatter; bescatter, bespatter, Mad Hatter.

-atter (-ŏ-). See **-otter.**

-attern, pattern, Saturn, slattern

-attle (-ă-), battle, cattle, chattel, prattle, rattle, tattle; embattle, Seattle; tittle-tattle.

-attle (-ŏ-). See **-ottle.**

-attler, battler, rattler, Statler, tattler.

-attling, battling, fatling, gatling, rattling, spratling, tattling.

-atto. See **-ateau.**

-atty, batty, chatty, fatty, gnatty, Hattie, matty, natty, patty, ratty.

-atum, datum, stratum; erratum, pomatum, substratum; postulatum, ultimatum; desideratum. See also **-atim.**

-ature (-ā-), nature; plicature; legislature, nomenclature.

-ature (-ă-). See **-atcher.**

-aturn. See **-attern.**

-atus (-ā-), status, stratus; afflatus, hiatus, senatus; apparatus, literatus.

-atus (-ă-), gratis, lattice, status; apparatus.

-aty, eighty, Haiti, Katie, matey, platy, praty, slaty, weighty.

-atyr. See **-atter.**

-audal. See **-awdle.**

-audit, audit, plaudit.

-audy. See **-awdy.**

-auger. See **-ager.**

-augher. See **-affer.**

-aughter (-ăf-). See **-after.**

-aughter (-ô-). See **-ater.**

-aughty, haughty, naughty.

-aulic, aulic; hydraulic; interaulic.

-aulter. See **-alter.**

-aulty. See **-alty.**

-aunder, launder, maunder.

-aunter, flaunter, gaunter, haunter, jaunter, saunter, taunter, vaunter.

-auntie. See **-anty.**

-auphin. See **-often.**

-aural. See **-oral.**

-aurel. See **-oral.**

-aurus. See **-orous.**

-auseous. See **-autious.**

-austral, austral, claustral.

-aution, caution; incaution, precaution.

-autious, cautious, nauseous; precautious.

-ava, brava, guava, Java, lava; cassava.

-avage, ravage, savage, scavage.

-avel, cavil, gavel, gravel, ravel, travail, travel; unravel.

-avelin, javelin, ravelin.

-aveling, knaveling, shaveling.

-avely, bravely, gravely, knavely, slavely, suavely.

-avement, lavement, pavement; depravement, engravement, enslavement.

-aven, craven, graven, haven, mavin, raven, shaven; engraven, New Haven.

-aver (-ā-), cadaver, palaver.

-aver (-ā-), braver, craver, favor, flavor, graver, haver, quaver, raver, savor, shaver, slaver, waiver, waver; disfavor, engraver, enslaver, papaver, lifesaver, timesaver; demiquaver, hemiquaver, semiquaver; hemidemisemi-quaver.

-avern, cavern, tavern.

-avid, avid, gravid, pavid; impavid.

-avior, clavier, pavior, savior, wavier, Xavier; behavior; misbehavior.

-avis, Davis, mavis; rara avis.

-avish (-ā-), bravish, knavish, slavish.

-avish (-ă-), lavish, ravish; enravish, MacTavish.

-avo, bravo, octavo.

-avor. See **-aver.**

-avy, cavy, Davy, gravy, navy, slavey, wavy; peccavi.

-awdle, caudal, dawdle.

-awdry, bawdry, tawdry.

-awdy, bawdy, dawdy, gaudy.

-awful, awful, lawful; unlawful.

-awning, awning, dawning, fawning, spawning, yawning.

-awny, brawny, fawny, lawny, Pawnee, scrawny, Shawnee, tawny, yawny; mulligatawny.

-awyer, foyer, lawyer, sawyer; topsawyer.

-axen, flaxen, Jackson, klaxon, Saxon, waxen; Anglo-Saxon.

-axi. See **-axy.**

-axon. See **-axen.**

-axy, flaxy, taxi, waxy; galaxy; ataraxy, Cotopaxi.

-aybe. See **-aby.**

-ayday, heyday, Mayday, payday, playday.

-ayer, layer, mayor, prayer; purveyor, soothsayer, surveyor.

    Also: **-ay** + **-er** (as in *player*, etc.)

-ayey, clayey, wheyey.

-aylay, Malay, melee, waylay; ukulele.

-ayling. See **-ailing.**

-ayman, Bremen, cayman, Damon, drayman, Haman, layman, Lehman, stamen; highwayman.

-ayment, claimant, payment, raiment; defrayment, displayment, repayment.

-ayo, kayo, Mayo.

-aza, Gaza, plaza; piazza.

-azard, hazard, mazzard; haphazard.

-azel. See **-asal**.

-azen. See **-azon**.

-azer, blazer, gazer, maser, phaser, praiser, razor; appraiser; paraphraser.

-azier, brazier, glazier, grazier.

-azon, blazon, brazen, glazen, raisin, scazon; emblazon; diapason.

-azzle, basil, dazzle, frazzle, razzle; bedazzle; razzle-dazzle.

-azy, crazy, daisy, hazy, lazy, Maisie, mazy.

-ea, Leah, zea; Althea, chorea, Crimea, idea, Judea, Korea, Maria, Medea, obeah, spirea; dahabeah, diarrhea, gonorrhea, Latakia, panacea, ratafia; Cassiopeia, cavalleria, pharmacopoeia; onomatopoeia.

-eaboard, keyboard, seaboard.

-eacher, beacher, bleacher, breacher, breecher, creature, feature, leacher, peacher, preacher, reacher, screecher, teacher; beseecher, impeacher.

-eachment, preachment; impeachment.

-eachy, beachy, litchi, Nietzsche, peachy, preachy, screechy.

-eacon, beacon, deacon, weaken; archdeacon.

-eaden, deaden, leaden, redden, threaden; Armageddon.

-eading. See **-edding**.

-eadle (-ē-). See **-eedle**.

-eadle (-ĕ-). See **-eddle**.

-eadlock, deadlock, headlock, wedlock.

-eadly, deadly, medley, redly.

-eady. See **-eedy**.

-eafer. See **-ephyr**.

-eager, eager, leaguer, meager; beleaguer, intriguer; overeager.

-eah. See **-ea.**

-eaken. See **-eacon.**

-eaker. See **-aker.**

-eakly, bleakly, meekly, sleekly, treacly, weakly, weekly; biweekly, obliquely, uniquely; semi-weekly.

-ealment, concealment, congealment, repealment, revealment.

-ealot. See **-ellate.**

-ealous, jealous, zealous; apellous, entellus, Marcellus, procellous, vitellus.

-ealy. See **-eely.**

-eamer, dreamer, emir, femur, lemur, reamer, schemer, steamer, streamer; blasphemer, redeemer.

-eamish, beamish, squeamish.

-eamster, deemster, seamster, teamster.

-ean, Ian, lien, paean; Aegean, Andean, astrean, Augean, Chaldean, Crimean, Judean, Korean, lethean, nymphean, pampean, plebian, plumbean, protean; amoebean, amphigean, apogean, Caribbean, empyrean, European, Galilean, gigantean, hymenean, Jacobean, Maccabean, perigean, phalangean, Tennessean; adamantean, antipodean, epicurean, terpsichorean.

-eaner, cleaner, gleaner, greener, meaner, wiener; demeanor, machiner; misdemeanor.

-eaning, gleaning, meaning.
    Also: **-ean** + **-ing** (as in *cleaning*, etc.)
    Also: **-een** + **-ing** (as in *preening*, etc.)
    Also: **-ene** + **-ing** (as in *intervening*, etc.)

    Also: **-ine** + **-ing** (as in *machining*, etc.)

-eanly, cleanly, keenly, leanly, meanly, queenly; obscenely, serenely.

-eanor. See **-eaner.**

-eany. See **-eeny.**

-eapen. See **-eepen.**

-eaper. See **-eeper.**

-earage. See **-eerage.**

-earance, clearance; appearance, arrearance, coherence, inherence; disappearance, incoherence, interference, perseverance.

-earful, cheerful, earful, fearful, sneerful.

-earing (-ĭr-), Bering, earring.
    Also: **-ear** + **-ing** (as in *hearing*, etc.)
    Also: **-eer** + **-ing** (as in *engineering*, etc.)
    Also: **-ere** + **-ing** (as in *adhering*, etc.)

-earing (-âr-). See **-aring.**

-earish. See **-arish.**

-early (-ĭr-). See **-erely.**

-early (-ûr-). See **-urly.**

-earner, burner, earner, learner; sojourner.

-earnest, earnest, Ernest, sternest; internist.

-earning, burning, earning, learning, spurning, turning, yearning; concerning, discerning, returning.

-earsal. See **-ersal.**

-earten. See **-arten.**

-eartener. See **-artner.**

-eartlet. See **-artlet.**

-earty. See **-arty.**

-eary, aerie, beery, bleary, cheery, dearie, dreary, eerie, Erie, jeery, leery, peri, query, smeary, sneery, sphery, veery, weary; aweary; miserere.

-easant, peasant, pheasant, pleasant, present; displeasant, unpleasant; omnipresent.

-easants. See **-esence.**

-easel, Diesel, easel, measle, teasel, weasel.

-easer, beezer, Caesar, easer, freezer, friezer, geezer, greaser, leaser, pleaser, sneezer, squeezer, teaser, tweezer, wheezer; Ebenezer.

-easing, breezing, easing, freezing, pleasing, sneezing, squeezing, teasing; appeasing, displeasing, unpleasing.

-eason, reason, season, treason, wizen; unreason.

-easoned, reasoned, seasoned, treasoned, weasand, wizened; unseasoned.

-easter, Easter, feaster; northeaster, southeaster.

-easting, bee-sting, easting, feasting.

-eastly, beastly, priestly.

-easure, leisure, measure, pleasure, treasure; admeasure, displeasure, entreasure, outmeasure.

-easy (-ē sǐ), creasy, fleecy, greasy.

-easy (-ē zǐ), breezy, cheesy, easy, freezy, greasy, queasy, sleazy, sneezy, wheezy; þarcheesi, speakeasy, uneasy, Zambezi.

-eaten, beaten, Cretan, cretin, eaten, Eton, heaten, sweeten, wheaten; moth-eaten, stormbeaten, unbeaten, worm-eaten; overeaten, weather-beaten.

-eater (-ē-), beater, cheater, eater, greeter, heater, liter, litre, meter, metre, neater, Peter, prætor, skeeter, sweeter, tweeter; beefeater, repeater, saltpeter, smoke-eater; centimeter, decimeter, kilometer, millimeter, overeater.

-eater (-ā-). See **-ator.**

-eather (-ē-), breather, either, neither, seether, sheather, wreather.

-eather (-ĕ-), blether, feather, heather, leather, nether, tether, weather, wether, whether; aweather, bellwether, pinfeather, together, whitleather; altogether.

-eathing, breathing, seething, sheathing, teething, wreathing; bequeathing.

-eatly. See -etely.

-eaty, meaty, peaty, sleety, sweetie, sweety, treaty; entreaty, Tahiti.

-eauty. See -ooty.

-eaven. See -even.

-eaver, beaver, cleaver, fever, griever, keever, lever, livre, reaver, riever, weaver, weever; achiever, believer, conceiver, deceiver, enfever, receiver; cantilever, Danny Deever, unbeliever.

-eavy. See -evy.

-eazy. See -easy.

-ebble, pebble, rebel, treble.

-ebel. See -ebble.

-eber. See -abor.

-eble. See -ebble.

-ebo, gazebo, placebo.

-ebtor. See -etter.

-ecant, piquant, precant, secant; cosecant; intersecant.

-ecca, Mecca; Rebecca.

-ecco. See -echo.

-ecent, decent, puissant, recent; indecent.

-echer. See -etcher.

-echo, echo, gecko, secco; El Greco, re-echo.

-ecian. See -etion.

-ecious, specious; facetious.

-ecis. See -acy.

-ecker, checker, chequer, wrecker; exchequer, woodpecker; double-decker, triple-decker.

-eckle, deckle, freckle, heckle, keckle, Seckel, shekel, speckle; bespeckle; Dr. Jekyll.

-eckless, feckless, fleckless, necklace, reckless, speckless.

-ecko. See -echo.

-eckon, beckon, reckon.

-eco. See -echo.

-econd, beckoned, fecund, reckoned, second.

-ectant, expectant, reflectent; disinfectant.

-ectar. See -ector.

-ecter. See -ector.

-ectful, neglectful, respectful; disrespectful.

-ectic, hectic, pectic; cachectic, eclectic; analectic, apoplectic, catalectic, dialectic.

-ectile, sectile; insectile, projectile.

-ection, flection, lection, section; affection, bisection, collection, complexion, confection, connection, convection, correction, defection, deflection, dejection, detection, direction, dissection, ejection, election, erection, infection, inflection, injection, inspection, objection, perfection, projection, protection, reflection, rejection, selection, subjection, subsection, trajection, trisection; circumspection, disaffection, disinfection, genuflexion, imperfection, indirection, insurrection, interjection, introspection, misdirection, predilection, recollection, re-election, resurrection, retrospection, venesection, vivisection.

-ective, sective; affective, collective, connective, corrective, defective, deflective, detective, directive, effective, elective, erective, infective, inflective, invective, neglective, objective, perfective, perspective, prospective, protective, reflective, rejective, respective, selective, subjective; ineffective, introspective, irrespective, retrospective.

-ectly, abjectly, correctly, directly, erectly; incorrectly, indirectly.

-ector, flector, hector, Hector, lector, nectar, rector, sector, specter, vector; collector, deflector, detector, director, ejecter, elector, injecter, inspector, objector, prospector, protector, reflector, selector.

-ecture, lecture, confecture, conjecture, prefecture, projecture; architecture.

-ecund. See **-econd.**

-edal (-ē-). See **-eddle.**

-edal (-ē-). See **-eedle.**

-edden. See **-eaden.**

-edding, bedding, dreading, heading, leading, redding, shedding, shredding, sledding, spreading, threading, wedding.

-eddle, heddle, medal, meddle, pedal, peddle, reddle, treadle; intermeddle.

-eddler, meddler, medlar, peddler, pedlar, treadler.

-eddy, eddy, Freddy, heady, ready, steady, Teddy; already, unready, unsteady.

-edence, credence; precedence; antecedence, intercedence.

-edent, credent, needn't, sedent; decedent, precedent; antecedent, intercedent.

-edger, dredger, edger, hedger, ledger, pledger, sledger.

-edic, Vedic; comedic; encyclopedic.

-edit, credit, edit; accredit, discredit, miscredit.

-edlar. See **-eddler.**

-edley. See **-eadly.**

-edo, credo, Lido; libido, stampedo, teredo, toledo, Toledo, torpedo, tuxedo.

-eecher. See **-eacher.**

-eecy. See **-easy.**

-eedful, deedful, heedful, needful; unheedful.

-eedle, beadle, needle, tweedle, wheedle; bipedal; centipedal, millepedal.

-eedling, needling, reedling, seedling, tweedling, wheedling.

-eedy, beady, deedy, greedy, heedy, needy, reedy, seedy, speedy, weedy; indeedy.

-eefy, beefy, leafy, reefy.

-eekly. See **-eakly.**

-eely, eely, freely, mealy, peely, really, seely, squealy, steely, wheely; genteelly.

-eeman, beeman, demon, freeman, gleeman, G-man, he-man, leman, seaman, semen.

-eemly. See **-emely.**

-eenly. See **-eanly.**

-eeny, genie, greeny, meanie, queenie, sheeny, Sweeney, teeny, weenie, weeny; Athene, Bellini, bikini, Bikini, Cellini, Houdini, martini, Puccini; Mussolini, Tetrazzini.

-eepen, cheapen, deepen, steepen.

-eeper, cheaper, creeper, deeper, keeper, leaper, peeper, reaper, sleeper, steeper, sweeper, Ypres.

-eeple. See **-ople.**

-eeply, cheaply, deeply.

    Also: **-eep** + **-ly** (as in *steeply*, etc.)

-eepsie. See **-ypsy.**

-eepy, creepy, sleepy, tepee, weepy.

-eerage, clearage, peerage, pierage, steerage; arrearage.

-eerful. See **-earful.**

-eerly. See **-erely.**

-eery. See **-eary.**

-eesi. See **-easy.**

-eesy. See **-easy.**

-eeten. See **-eaten.**

-eeter. See **-eater.**

-eether. See **-eather.**

-eetle, beetle, betel, fetal; decretal.

-eetly. See **-etely.**

-eety. See **-eaty.**

-eever. See **-eaver.**

-eevish, peevish, thievish.

-eezer. See **-easer.**

-eezing. See **-easing.**

-eezy. See **-easy.**

-egal, eagle, beagle, legal, regal; illegal, vice-regal.

-eggar, beggar, egger; bootlegger.

-eggy, dreggy, eggy, leggy, Peggy.

-egian. See **-egion.**

-egion, legion, region; collegian, Glaswegian, Norwegian.

-egious. See **-igious.**

-egnant, pregnant, regnant; impregnant.

-egress, egress, Negress, regress.

-eifer. See **-ephyr.**

-eighbor. See **-abor.**

-einty. See **-ainty.**

-einy. See **-ainy.**

-eiress. See **-aris.**

-eisance. See **-ascence.**

-eist, deist, seest, theist.

-eisure. See **-easure.**

-eiter. See **-itter.**

-either (-ī-). See **-ither.**

-either (-ē-). See **-eather.**

-eiver. See **-eaver.**

-ekyll. See **-eckle.**

-elate, helot, pellet, prelate, stellate, zealot; constellate; interpellate.

-elder, elder, gelder, melder, welder.

-elding, gelding, melding, welding.

-eldom, beldam, seldom.

-ele. See **-alely.**

-elee. See **-aylay.**

-elfish, elfish, pelfish, selfish, shellfish; unselfish.

-elic, bellic, melic, relic, telic; angelic; archangelic, evangelic, philatelic.

-eline, beeline, feline.

-elion, Pelion; aphelion, chameleon, Mendelian; perihelion.

-elix, Felix, helix.

-ella, Bella, Ella, fella, Stella; capella, Louella, patella, umbrella; Cinderella, Isabella, tarantella.

-ellar. See **-eller.**

-ellen. See **-elon.**

-eller, cellar, dweller, feller, heller, seller, smeller, speller, stellar, teller; impeller, propeller, saltcellar; fortune teller, interstellar.

-ellet. See **-elate.**

-elli. See -elly.

-ellish, hellish, relish; embellish.

-ello, bellow, cello, felloe, fellow, hello, Jello, mellow, yellow; duello, good fellow, niello; brocatello, Donatello, Monticello, punchinello, saltarello; violoncello.

-ellous. See -ealous.

-ellow. See -ello.

-ellum, vellum; flagellum; ante-bellum, cerebellum.

-ellus. See -ealous.

-elly, belly, Delhi, felly, helly, jelly, Kelly, Nellie, Shelley, shelly, smelly; cancelli, rakehelly; Botticelli, Donatelli, vermicelli; Machiavelli.

-elon, Ellen, felon, Helen, melon; watermelon.

-elop, develop, envelop.

-elot. See -ellate.

-elter, belter, felter, kelter, melter, pelter, shelter, smelter, spelter, swelter, welter; helter-skelter.

-elving, delving, helving, shelving.

-eman. See -eeman.

-ember, ember, member; December, dismember, November, remember, September; disremember.

-emble, semble, tremble; assemble, dissemble; reassemble.

-embly, trembly; assembly.

-emely, seemly; extremely, supremely, unseemly.

-emer. See -eamer.

-emic, chemic; alchemic, endemic, pandemic, polemic, systemic, totemic; academic, epidemic, theoremic.

-emish, blemish, Flemish.

-emlin, gremlin, Kremlin.

-emma, Emma, gemma; dilemma.

-emner. See **-emor.**

-emon. See **-eeman.**

-emor, hemmer, tremor; condemner, contemner.

-emplar, templar; exemplar.

-empter, tempter; attempter, exempter, preempter.

-emption, emption; ademption, coemption, diremption, exemption, pre-emption, redemption.

-emur. See **-eamer.**

-ena. See **-ina.**

-enace. See **-ennis.**

-enal, penal, renal, venal; adrenal, machinal.

-enant, pennant, tenant; lieutenant.

-enate. See **-ennet.**

-enceforth, henceforth, thenceforth.

-encer. See **-enser.**

-encher, bencher, blencher, censure, clencher, denture, quencher, trencher, venture, wencher; adventure, debenture, indenture; misadventure, peradventure.

-enchman, Frenchman, henchman.

-encil, mensal, pencil, pensil, pensile, stencil, tensile; extensile, prehensile, utensil.

-enda, Brenda, Zenda; addenda, agenda, credenda, delenda, corrigenda, hacienda.

-endance. See **-endence.**

-endant. See **-endent.**

-endence, tendance; ascendance, attendance, dependence, impendence, resplendence, transcendence; condescendence, independence; interdependence.

-endent, pendant, pendent, splendent; appendant, ascendant, attendant, contendent, defendant, dependant, dependent, descendant, descendent, impendent, intendant, resplendent, transcendent, transplendent; independent; interdependent, superintendent.

-ender, bender, blender, fender, gender, lender, render, sender, slender, spender, splendor, tender, vendor; amender, contender, defender, emender, engender, offender, perpender, pretender, surrender, suspender, week-ender.

-ending, ending, pending.

　　Also: **-end** + **-ing** (as in *ascending*, etc.)

-endor. See **-ender.**

-endous, horrendous, stupendous, tremendous.

-endum, addendum, agendum, credendum; corrigendum, referendum.

-enely. See **-eanly.**

-enet. See **-ennet.**

-engthen, lengthen, strengthen.

-enial, genial, menial, venial; congenial.

-enic, phrenic, scenic, splenic; arsenic, eugenic, Hellenic, irenic; calisthenic, neurasthenic, pathogenic, photogenic, psychogenic, telegenic.

-enie. See **-ainy.**

-enim. See **-enum.**

-enin. See **-enon.**

-enish, plenish, Rhenish, wennish; replenish.

-enna, henna, senna; antenna, duenna, Gehenna, Ravenna, Siena, sienna, Vienna.

-ennant. See **-enant**.

-ennel, fennel, kennel, antennal.

-enner. See **-enor**.

-ennet, Bennett, jennet, rennet, senate, tenet.

-ennis, Dennis, menace, tenace, tennis, Venice.

-enny, any, Benny, Denny, fenny, jenny, Jenny, Kenny, Lenny, many, penny, tenney, wenny, Kilkenny.

-eno, keno, Reno, Zeno; bambino, casino, merino; Filipino, maraschino.

-enom. See **-enum**.

-enon, Lenin, pennon, tenon.

-enor, penner, tenor, tenour.

-ensely, densely, tensely; immensely, intensely.

-enser, censer, censor, denser, fencer, Spencer, Spenser, tensor; commencer, condenser, dispenser, extensor, intenser.

-ensil. See **-encil**.

-ensile. See **-encil**.

-ension. See **-ention**.

-ensive, pensive, tensive; ascensive, defensive, distensive, expensive, extensive, intensive, offensive, ostensive, protensive, suspensive, apprehensive, comprehensive, indefensive, inexpensive, influencive, inoffensive, recompensive, reprehensive; incomprehensive.

-ensor. See **-enser**.

-enta, magenta, placenta, polenta.

-ental, cental, dental, gentle, lentil, mental, rental, trental; fragmental, parental, pigmental, placental, segmental, tridental, accidental, alimental, complemental, complimental, continental, departmental, detrimental, elemental, fundamental, governmental, incidental, instrumental, ligamental, monumental, Occidental, Oriental, ornamental, regimental, rudimental, sacramental, supplemental, testamental, transcendental; coincidental, developmental, experimental, impedimental, labiodental, temperamental, transcontinental; intercontinental.

-entance, sentence, repentance; unrepentance.

-entence. See -entance.

-enter, center, enter, lentor, mentor, renter, tenter; dissenter, frequenter, inventor, lamenter, off-center, precentor, re-enter, repenter, tormentor; experimenter.

-entful, eventful, repentful, resentful; uneventful.

-ential, agential, credential, essential, potential, prudential, sentential, sequential, tangential, torrential; confidential, consequential, deferential, differential, evidential, existential, exponential, inferential, influential, penitential, pestilential, precedential, preferential, presidential, providential, quintessential, referential, reverential, unessential; experiential, inconsequential.

entic, authentic, identic.

enticed. See -entist.

entil. See -ental.

-entile, gentile; percentile.

-entin, dentin, Lenten, Trenton; San Quentin.

-enting, denting, renting, scenting, tenting, venting; absenting, accenting, assenting, augmenting, cementing, consenting, fermenting, fomenting, frequenting, lamenting, presenting, preventing, relenting, resenting, tormenting; circumventing, complimenting, ornamenting, representing, supplementing; misrepresenting.

-ention, gentian, mention, pension, tension; abstention, ascension, attention, contention, convention, declension, detention, dimension, dissension, distension, extension, intension, intention, invention, prehension, pretension, prevention, propension, recension, retention, subvention, suspension; apprehension, circumvention, comprehension, condescension, contravention, inattention, intervention, reprehension; incomprehension, misapprehension.

-entious, contentious, dissentious, licentious, pretentious, sententious, silentious; conscientious, pestilentious.

-entist, dentist, prenticed; Adventist, apprenticed, preventist.

-entive, assentive, attentive, incentive, presentive, retentive; inattentive.

-entle. See **-ental.**

-ently, gently; intently; evidently.

-entment, contentment, presentment, relentment, resentment; discontentment, representment.

-ento, cento, lento; memento, pimento; Sacramento.

-entor, centaur, mentor, stentor; succentor.

-entor. See **-enter.**

-entous, momentous, portentous.

-entric, centric; acentric, concentric, eccentric, geocentric; anthropocentric, heliocentric.

-entry, entry, gentry, sentry.

-enture. See -encher.

-enty, plenty, scenty, twenty; cognoscenti;
  Agua Caliente, dolce far niente.

-enu, menu, venue.

-enum, denim, frenum, plenum, venom.

-eny. See -ainy.

-enza, cadenza; influenza.

-eo, Cleo, Leo, Rio, trio.

-eomen. See -omen.

-eon, aeon, Creon, Leon, neon, paean, peon;
  pantheon; Anacreon.

-eopard, jeopard, leopard, peppered, shepherd.

-eople, people, steeple; unpeople.

-epee. See -eepy.

-epherd. See -eopard.

-ephyr, deafer, feoffor, heifer, zephyr.

-epid, tepid, trepid; intrepid.

-epper, leper, pepper, stepper; high-stepper.

-epsy, Pepsi; apepsy, eupepsy; catalepsy,
  epilepsy.

-eptic, peptic, septic, skeptic; aseptic, dispeptic,
  eupeptic; antiseptic, cataleptic, epileptic.

-era, era, Vera; chimera; Halmahera.

-erance. See -earance.

-ercer. See -urser.

-ercion. See -ertion.

-erder. See -urder.

-erdure. See -erger.

-erely, cheerly, clearly, dearly, merely, nearly,
  queerly, sheerly, yearly; austerely, severely,
  sincerely; cavalierly, insincerely.

-erence. See -earance.

-ergeant. See -argent.

-ergence, convergence, divergence, emergence, resurgence, submergence.

-ergent, turgent, urgent, vergent; abstergent, assurgent, convergent, detergent, divergent, emergent, insurgent, resurgent.

-erger, merger, perjure, purger, scourger, splurger, urger, verdure, verger; converger, diverger, emerger, submerger.

-ergy. See **-urgy.**

-eri. See **-erry.**

-eric, cleric, Derek, derrick, Eric, ferric, Herrick, spheric; chimeric, enteric, generic, Homeric, hysteric, mesmeric, numeric, suberic, valeric; atmospheric, chromospheric, climacteric, esoteric, exoteric, hemispheric, isomeric, neoteric, peripheric, phylacteric.

-eries, dearies, queries, series, wearies.

-eril, beryl, Merrill, peril, sterile.

-erile. See **-eril.**

-erish, cherish, perish.

-erit, ferret, merit; demerit, inherit; disinherit.

-erjure. See **-erger.**

-erker. See **-irker.**

-erky, jerky, murky, perky, turkey.

-erkin, firkin, gherkin, jerkin, merkin, Perkin.

-erling. See **-urling.**

-erly. See **-urly.**

-ermal, dermal, thermal.

-erman, Burman, firman, German, Herman, merman, sermon. See also **-ermine.**

-erment, ferment; affirmant, averment, deferment, determent, interment, preferment, referment; disinterment.

-ermes, Burmese, fermis, Hermes.

-ermine, ermine, vermin; determine; predetermine. See also **-erman.**

-ermy, fermi, Nurmi, squirmy, wormy; diathermy, taxidermy.

-ernal, colonel, journal, kernel, sternal, urnal, vernal; cavernal, diurnal, eternal, external, fraternal, hibernal, infernal, internal, lucernal, maternal, nocturnal, paternal, supernal; co-eternal, hodiernal, sempiternal.

-ernest. See **-earnest.**

-erning. See **-earning.**

-ernist. See **-earnest.**

-erno, Sterno; inferno.

-ero (-ē-), hero, Nero, zero.

-ero (-â-). See **-arrow.**

-errand, errand, gerund.

-errant, errant, gerent; aberrant, knight-errant, vicegerent.

-errick. See **-eric.**

-errier, burier, merrier, terrier.

-erring, derring, erring, herring.

-error, error, terror.

-errot. See **-arrow.**

-erry, berry, bury, cherry, Derry, ferry, Jerry, Kerry, merry, Perry, sherry, skerry, Terry, very, wherry; Bambury, blackberry, blueberry, cranberry, gooseberry, mulberry, raspberry, strawberry; beriberi, boysenberry, capillary, cemetery, culinary, elderberry, huckleberry, Janissary, lamasery, loganberry, millinery, monastery, Pondicherry, presbytery, stationary, stationery. See also **-ary.**

-ersal, bursal, tercel, versal; rehearsal, reversal, transversal, universal.

-ersey, furzy, jersey, Jersey, kersey.

-ersian. See **-ersion.**

-ersion, Persian, version; abstersion, aspersion, aversion, conversion, discursion, dispersion, diversion, emersion, excursion, immersion, incursion, inversion, perversion, recursion, reversion, submersion, subversion; extroversion, introversion; animadversion.

-erson, person, worsen.

-ertain, Burton, certain, curtain, Merton; uncertain.

-erter, blurter, curter, flirter, hurter, squirter; asserter, averter, converter, deserter, diverter, exerter, inserter, inverter, perverter, subverter.

-ertie. See **-irty.**

-ertile. See **-urtle.**

-ertion, tertian, version; assertion, coercion, desertion, exertion, insertion; disconcertion.

-ertive, furtive; assertive, divertive, exertive, revertive.

-ertly, curtly, pertly; alertly, expertly; inertly, invertly, overtly; inexpertly.

-erule, ferule, ferrule, perule, spherule.

-ervant, curvant, fervent, servant; conservant, observant, recurvant; unobservant.

-ervent. See **-ervant.**

-erver, fervor, nerver, server, swerver; conserver, observer, preserver, reserver, timeserver.

-ervid, fervid; perfervid, scurvied.

-ervish, dervish, nervish.

-ervy. See **-urvy.**

-ery. See **-erry.**

-escence, essence; excresence, florescence, pubescence, putrescence, quiescence, quintessence, rubescence, senescence, tumescence, vitrescence; acquiescence, adolescence, coalescence, convalescence, deliquescence, effervescence, efflorescence, evanescence, fluorescence, incalescence, incandescence, iridescence, obsolescence, opalescence, phosphorescence, recrudescence.

-escent, cessant, crescent, jessant; depressant, excrescent, ignescent, incessant, liquescent, putrescent, quiescent, rubescent, senescent; adolescent, convalescent, deliquescent, effervescent, efflorescent, evanescent, fluorescent, incandescent, obsolescent, opalescent, phosphorescent, recrudescent.

-escience, nescience, prescience.

-escue, fescue, rescue; Montesquieu.

-esence, pleasance, presence; omnipresence.
  Also: -easant + -s (as in *peasants*, etc.)

-esent. See -easant.

-eshen. See -ession.

-esher, fresher, pressure, thresher; refresher.

-eshly, fleshly, freshly.

-eshy, fleshy, meshy.

-esian. See -esion.

-esion, lesion; adhesion, artesian, Cartesian, cohesion, Ephesian, Parisian, Silesian; Indonesian, Micronesian, Polynesian.

-esis, Croesus, rhesus, thesis, tmesis; mimesis; catachresis, exegesis; aposiopesis.

-essage, dressage, message, presage; expressage.

-essal. See -estle.

-essant. See -escent.

-essel. See -estle.

-essence. See -escence.

-esser. See -essor.

-essful, distressful, successful; unsuccessful.

-essie. See -essy.

-essing, blessing, dressing, guessing, pressing.
Also: **-ess** + **-ing** (as in *depressing*, etc.)
Also: **-esce** + **-ing** (as in *convalescing*, etc.)

-ession, cession, freshen, Hessian, session;
accession, aggression, bull session, compression, concession, confession, depression, digression, discretion, expression, impression, ingression, obsession, oppression, possession, precession, procession, profession, progression, recession, secession, succession, suppression, transgression; indiscretion, intercession, prepossession, retrocession, retrogression, supersession.

-essive, aggressive, compressive, concessive, depressive, digressive, excessive, expressive, impressive, oppressive, possessive, progressive, recessive, regressive, repressive, successive, suppressive, transgressive; retrogressive.

-essor, dresser, guesser, lesser, lessor, presser; addresser, aggressor, assessor, compressor, confessor, depressor, oppressor, possessor, professor, successor, suppressor, transgressor; antecessor, intercessor, predecessor, second-guesser, tongue-depressor.

-essure. See -esher.

-essy, Bessie, dressy, Jessie, messy, Tessie, tressy.

-esta, celesta, fiesta, siesta.

-estal, festal, vestal.

-ester, Chester, ester, Esther, fester, Hester, jester, Leicester, Lester, Nestor, pester, tester, vester, wrester; Chichester, Colchester, digester, Dorchester, Eastchester, investor, Manchester, nor'wester, protester, semester, sequester, sou'wester, Sylvester, trimester, Westchester; midsemester.

-estial, bestial, celestial.

-estic, domestic, majestic; anapestic, catachrestic.

-estine, destine; clandestine, intestine, predestine.

-estive, festive, restive; attestive, congestive, digestive, suggestive, tempestive.

-estle, Cecil, nestle, pestle, trestle, vessel; Horst Wessel, redressal.

-estler, nestler, wrestler.

-esto, presto; manifesto.

-estos, cestus; asbestos.

-estral, kestrel; ancestral, fenestral, orchestral, trimestral.

-esture, gesture; divesture, investure.

-esty, chesty, cresty, resty, testy.

-esus. See **-esis**.

-etail, detail, retail.

-etal. See **-ettle**.

-etcher, etcher, fetcher, fletcher, lecher, retcher, sketcher, stretcher.

-etchy, fetchy, sketchy, stretchy, tetchy, vetchy.

-ete. See **-etty**.

-etely, fleetly, meetly, neatly, sweetly; com-

pletely, concretely, discreetly; incompletely,
indiscreetly, obsoletely.

-eter. See **-eater.**

-etful, fretful; forgetful, regretful.

-ethel, Bethel, Ethel, ethyl, methyl.

-ether. See **-eather.**

-ethyl. See **-ethel.**

-etic, aesthetic, ascetic, athletic, cosmetic,
emetic, frenetic, genetic, hermetic, kinetic,
magnetic, mimetic, pathetic, phonetic, phre-
netic, poetic, prophetic, splenetic, synthetic;
abietic, alphabetic, anaesthetic, antithetic,
apathetic, arithmetic, dietetic, energetic, exe-
getic, geodetic, homiletic, hypothetic, maso-
retic, parenthetic, sympathetic, theoretic;
antipathetic, biogenetic, peripatetic; abio-
genetic; onomatopoetic.

-etion (-ē-), Grecian; accretion, completion,
concretion, deletion, depletion, excretion,
repletion, secretion.

-etion (-ĕ-). See **-ession.**

-etious. See **-ecious.**

-etish. See **-ettish.**

-eto, Tito, veto; bonito, mosquito.

-etor. See **-etter.**

-etsy, Betsy, tsetse.

-etter, better, bettor, debtor, fetter, getter, letter,
setter, wetter, whetter; abettor, begetter,
forgetter, go-getter, typesetter, unfetter;
carburetor.

-etti. See **-etty.**

-ettish, fetish, Lettish, pettish, wettish; coquet-
tish.

-ettle, fettle, Gretel, kettle, metal, mettle, nettle,

petal, settle; abettal, unsettle; Popocatapetl.

-etto, ghetto, petto; falsetto, libretto, palmetto, stiletto, terzetto, zuchetto; allegretto, lazaretto, Rigoletto.

-ettor. See **-etter.**

-etty (-ĕ-), Betty, fretty, Hetty, jetty, Lettie, netty, petit, petty, sweaty; confetti, libretti, machete, Rossetti, spaghetti; Donizetti, spermaceti.

-etty (-ĭ-). See **-itty.**

-etus, fetus; quietus.

-euced. See **-ucid.**

-eudal. See **-oodle.**

-eudo. See **-udo.**

-eum, lyceum, museum, Te Deum; atheneum, colosseum, mausoleum; peritoneum.

-eura. See **-ura.**

-eural. See **-ural.**

-euter. See **-ooter.**

-eutic, scorbutic; pharmaceutic, therapeutic.

-eutist. See **-utist.**

-eval. See **-evil.**

-evel, bevel, devil, level, Neville, revel; bedevil, dishevel.

-even (-ĕ-), Devon, heaven, leaven, seven; eleven, replevin.

-even (-ē-), even, Stephen, Steven; uneven.

-ever (-ĕ-), clever, ever, lever, never, sever; assever, dissever, endeavor, however, whatever, whenever, wherever, whichever, whoever, whomever; howsoever, whatsoever, whencesoever, whensoever, wheresoever, whomsoever, whosoever.

-ever (-ē-). See **-eaver.**

-evil (-ē-), evil, weevil; coeval, primeval, retrieval, upheaval; medieval.

-evil (-ĕ-). See **-evel.**

-evious, devious, previous.

-evy, bevy, Chevy, heavy, levee, levy; top-heavy.

-ewal. See **-uel.**

-eward, leeward, sewered, skewered, steward.

-ewdest. See **-udist.**

-ewdish. See **-udish.**

-ewdly. See **-udely.**

-ewel. See **-uel.**

-ewess, Lewis, Louis, Jewess.

-ewish, blueish, Jewish, newish, shrewish, truish.

-ewly. See **-uly.**

-ewry. See **-ury.**

-ewsy. See **-oozy.**

-ewy, bluey, buoy, chewy, cooee, dewy, fluey, gluey, gooey, hooey, Louie, Louis, pfui, screwy, thewy, viewy; chop suey.

-exas. See **-exus.**

-exer, flexor, vexer; annexer, perplexer.

-exile, exile, flexile.

-extant, extant, sextant.

-extile, sextile, textile; bissextile.

-exus, nexus, plexus, Texas; Alexis; solar plexus.

-exy, prexy, sexy; apoplexy.

-eyance, seance; abeyance, conveyance, purveyance.

-eyor. See **-ayer.**

-eyrie. See **-ary.**

-ezi. See **-easy.**

-ia. See **-ea.**

-iad, dryad, naiad, triad; jeremiad.

-ial, dial, phial, trial, vial, viol; decrial, denial, espial, retrial, sundial, supplial.

-iam, Priam, Siam; Omar Khayyam.

-ian. See **-ion.**

-iance, clients, giants, science; affiance, alliance, appliance, compliance, defiance, reliance, suppliance; misalliance.

-iant, client, giant, pliant, scient; affiant, compliant, defiant, reliant.

-iants. See **-iance.**

-iaper. See **-iper.**

-iar. See **-ier.**

-iary. See **-iry.**

-ias, bias, pious; Elias, Tobias; Ananias, nisi prius.

-iat. See **-iet.**

-ibal. See **-ible.**

-ibald. See **-ibbled.**

-ibber, bibber, cribber, dibber, fibber, gibber, glibber, jibber, nibber, squibber; ad-libber, winebibber.

-ibbet. See **-ibit.**

-ibble, cribble, dibble, dribble, fribble, kibble, nibble, quibble, scribble, sibyl, Sybil, thribble; ish-kabibble.

-ibbled, dibbled, dribbled, kibbled, nibbled, piebald, quibbled, ribald, scribbled.

-ibbling, dibbling, dribbling, nibbling, quibbling, scribbling, sibling.

-ibbly, dribbly, fribbly, glibly, nibbly, quibbly, scribbly, tribbly.

-ibbon, gibbon, ribbon.

-ibel. See **-ible.**

-iber, briber, fiber, giber, Tiber; imbiber,

inscriber, prescriber, subscriber, transcriber.

-ibit, gibbet, Tibbett, zibet; cohibit, exhibit, inhibit, prohibit.

-ible, Bible, libel, tribal.

-iblet, driblet, giblet, triblet.

-ibling. See **-ibbling.**

-ibyl. See **-ibble.**

-ica, mica, Micah, pica.

-icar. See **-icker.**

-icely. See **-isely.**

-icial, comitial, initial, judicial, official; artificial, beneficial, interstitial, prejudicial, sacrificial, superficial.

-ician. See **-ition.**

-icient, deficient, efficient, omniscient, proficient, sufficient; coefficient, inefficient, insufficient.

-icious, vicious; ambitious, auspicious, capricious, delicious, factitious, fictitious, judicious, malicious, nutritious, officious, pernicious, propitious, seditious, suspicious; adventitious, avaricious, expeditious, inauspicious, injudicious, meretricious, superstitious, suppositious, surreptitious.

-icken, chicken, quicken, sicken, stricken, thicken, wicken.

-icker, bicker, dicker, flicker, kicker, knicker, licker, liquor, picker, quicker, sicker, slicker, snicker, thicker, ticker, vicar, wicker.

-icket, clicket, cricket, picket, piquet, pricket, thicket, ticket, wicket.

-ickle, chicle, fickle, mickle, nickel, pickle, prickle, sickle, stickle, strickle, tickle, trickle.

-ickly, prickly, quickly, sickly, slickly, thickly, trickly.

-ickset, quickset, thickset.

-ickshaw, kickshaw, rickshaw.

-icky, dickey, Dicky, Mickey, Nicky, quickie, rickey, sticky, thicky, tricky, Vicki; doo-hickey, Kon-tiki.

-icle. See -ickle.

-icon. See -iken.

-icter, lictor, stricter, victor; afflicter, conflicter, constrictor, inflicter, predicter; contradicter; boa constrictor.

-iction, diction, fiction, friction; addiction, affliction, confliction, constriction, conviction, depiction, eviction, infliction, prediction, reliction, restriction, transfixion; benediction, contradiction, dereliction, interdiction, jurisdiction, malediction, valediction.

-ictive, fictive; afflictive, conflictive, constrictive, inflictive, predictive, restrictive, vindictive; benedictive, contradictive, interdictive, jurisdictive.

-ictor. See -icter.

-ictualler. See -ittler.

-icture, picture, stricture; depicture.

-ictus, ictus; Benedictus.

-icy, icy, spicy.

-idal, bridal, bridle, idle, idol, idyl, sidle, tidal; fratricidal, homicidal, matricidal, parricidal, regicidal, suicidal; infanticidal, tyrannicidal.

-idden, bidden, chidden, hidden, midden, ridden, slidden, stridden; hag-ridden, unbidden.

-iddle, diddle, fiddle, griddle, piddle, quiddle, riddle, tiddle, twiddle.

-iddling, fiddling, kidling, middling, piddling, riddling, twiddling.

-iddy, biddy, giddy, kiddie, middy, stiddy.

-iden, guidon, Haydn, Leyden, widen; Poseidon.

-ident, bident, rident, strident, trident.

-ider, cider, eider, glider, guider, hider, rider, spider, wider; backslider, confider, divider, insider, outrider, outsider, provider.

-idget, Bridget, digit, fidget, midget.

-idgy, midgy, ridgy.

-idle. See **-idal.**

-idly, idly, widely.

-idney, kidney, Sidney.

-ido. See **-edo.**

-idol. See **-idal.**

-idy, sidy, tidy; untidy; bona fide.

-idyl. See **-idal.**

-iefly, briefly, chiefly.

-ience. See **-iance.**

-ient. See **-iant.**

-ients. See **-iance.**

-ier, briar, brier, buyer, drier, dyer, flier, friar, fryer, higher, liar, mire, nigher, plier, prior, pryer, shyer, sigher, slyer, spryer, spyer, tire, Tyre, vier.

Also: **-y** + **-er** (as in *amplifier*, etc.)

See also: **-ire.**

-iery. See **-iry.**

-iestly. See **-eastly.**

-iet, diet, fiat, quiet, riot, striate; disquiet.

-ieval. See **-evil.**

-iever. See **-eaver.**

-ifer, cipher, fifer, knifer, lifer, rifer; decipher.

-iffin, biffin, griffin, griffon, stiffen, tiffin.

-iffle, piffle, riffle, sniffle, whiffle.

-iffy, iffy, jiffy, sniffy, spiffy.

-ific, glyphic; deific, horrific, pacific, pontific, prolific, somnific, specific, terrific; beatific, calorific, hieroglyphic, honorific, humorific, scientific, soporific.

-ifle, Eiffel, eyefull, rifle, stifle, trifle.

-ifling, rifling, stifling, trifling.

-ifter, drifter, grifter, lifter, shifter, sifter, swifter; shoplifter, uplifter.

-iftless, driftless, shiftless, thriftless.

-ifty, clifty, drifty, fifty, nifty, rifty, shifty, thrifty.

-igate. See -igot.

-iggard. See -iggered.

-igger, bigger, chigger, digger, figger, jigger, rigger, rigor, swigger, trigger, twigger, vigor; gold digger, grave digger, outrigger.

-iggered, figgered, jiggered, niggard.

-iggle, giggle, higgle, jiggle, niggle, sniggle, squiggle, wiggle, wriggle.

-iggly, bigly, giggly, sniggly, wriggly; piggly-wiggly.

-igher. See -ier.

-ighland. See -island.

-ighly. See -ily.

-ighness. See -inus.

-ighten, brighten, Brighton, frighten, heighten, lighten, tighten, Titan, triton, whiten; enlighten.

-ightening, brightening, frightening, lightning, tightening, whitening.

-ighter, biter, blighter, brighter, fighter, kiter, lighter, miter, niter, tighter, titer, triter, writer; backbiter, first-nighter, igniter, inciter, inditer, moonlighter, prize fighter, type-writer; copywriter, dynamiter, underwriter.

-ightful, frightful, mightful, rightful, spiteful, sprightful; delightful.

-ighting. See **-iting.**

-ightly, brightly, knightly, lightly, nightly, sprightly, tightly, tritely; politely, unsightly; impolitely.

-ightning. See **-ightening.**

-ighty, blighty, flighty, mighty, mitey, nightie, whitey; almighty; Aphrodite.

-igil, sigil, strigil, vigil.

-igious, litigious, prodigious, religious; irre-ligious, sacrilegious.

-igit. See **-idget.**

-igly. See **-iggly.**

-igma, sigma, stigma; enigma.

-igment, figment, pigment.

-ignant, benignant, indignant, malignant.

-igner. See **-iner.**

-ignly. See **-inely.**

-ignment, alignment, assignment, confinement, consignment, designment, entwinement, in-clinement, refinement, resignment.

-igor. See **-igger.**

-igot, bigot, frigate, gigot, spigot.

-iguer. See **-eager.**

-iken, icon, lichen, liken.

-iking, biking, diking, hiking, liking, piking, spiking, striking, Viking; disliking.

-ila. See **-illa.**

-ilbert, filbert, Gilbert.

-ilding. See **-uilding.**

-ildish, childish, mildish, wildish.

-ildly, childly, mildly, wildly.

-i?dor. See **-uilder.**

-ile. See **-illy.**

-ilely. See **-ily.**

-ili. See **-illy.**

-ilian. See **-illion.**

-ilient. See **-illiant.**

-ilight, highlight, skylight, twilight.

-ilious, bilious; punctilious; atrabilious, supercilious.

-ilken, milken, silken.

-ilky, milky, silky, Willkie.

-illa, Scylla, villa; cedilla, chinchilla, flotilla, gorilla, guerrilla, manila, Manila, mantilla, Priscilla, vanilla; camarilla, cascarilla, sabadilla, sequidilla, sarsaparilla.

-illful, skillful, willful; unskillful.

-illian. See **-illion.**

-illie. See **-illy.**

-illion, billion, Lillian, million, pillion, trillion; carillon, Castilian, civilian, cotillon, pavilion, postilion, quadrillion, Quintilian, quintillion, reptilian, vermilion; Maximilian.

-illage, grillage, pillage, tillage, village.

-iller, chiller, driller, filler, griller, killer, miller, pillar, Schiller, spiller, swiller, thriller, tiller; distiller, Joe Miller, maxillar; caterpillar, killer-diller, ladykiller.

-illes. See **-illies.**

-illet, billet, fillet, millet, rillet, skillet.

-illiant, brilliant; resilient.

-illiard, billiard, milliard, mill-yard.

-illie. See **-illy.**

-illies, fillies, gillies, lilies, willies; Achilles, Antilles.

-illing, billing, shilling, willing; unwilling. Also: **-ill** + **-ing** (as in *filling*, etc.)

-illo. See **-illow.**

-illow, billow, kilo, pillow, willow; negrillo; armadillo, peccadillo.

-illy, billy, Billy, Chile, chili, chilly, filly, frilly, gillie, grilly, hilly, illy, killi, lily, Lily, Millie, Phily, shrilly, silly, stilly, Tillie, Willie; Piccadilly, piccalilli, tiger lily, water lily, willy-nilly; daffy-down-dilly.

-ilo. See **-illow.**

-ilot, eyelet, islet, pilot.

-ilter, filter, jilter, kilter, milter, philter, quilter, tilter, wilter.

-ilton, Hilton, Milton, Stilton, Wilton.

-ily (-ī-), drily, highly, Reilly, Riley, shyly, slyly, vilely, wily, wryly; O'Reilly, servilely.

-ily (-ĭ-). See **-illy.**

-image, image, scrimmage.

-imate, climate, primate; acclimate.

-imber, limber, timber, timbre; unlimber.

-imble, cymbal, fimble, Gimbel, nimble, symbol, thimble, tymbal, wimble.

-imbo, kimbo, limbo; akimbo.

-imely, primely, timely; sublimely, untimely.

-imen. See **-imon.**

-imer. See **-immer.**

-imey. See **-imy.**

-imic, chymic, mimic; alchymic, cherubimic, eponymic, homonymic, metonymic, metronymic, pantomimic, patronymic, synonymic.

-iming, chiming, climbing, liming, priming, rhyming, timing.

-imly, dimly, grimly, primly, trimly.

-immer, brimmer, dimmer, glimmer, grimmer, primer, shimmer, simmer, skimmer, slimmer, swimmer, trimmer.

-imming, brimming, dimming, skimming, slimming, swimming, trimming.

-immy, gimme, jimmy, Jimmy, shimmy.

-imon, Hyman, Hymen, limen, pieman, Simon.

-imper, crimper, limper, scrimper, shrimper, simper, whimper.

-imple, crimple, dimple, pimple, rimple, simple, wimple.

-imply, crimply, dimply, limply, pimply, simply.

-impy, impy, scrimpy.

-imsy, flimsy, mimsy, whimsy.

-imy, blimey, grimy, limey, limy, rimy, slimy, stymie, thymy.

-ina (-ē-), Gina, Lena, Nina, scena, Tina; arena, catena, Christina, czarina, farina, galena, Helena, hyena, Katrina, maizena, Regina, subpoena, tsarina, verbena; Argentina, cavatina, concertina, ocarina, Pasadena, philopena, scarlatina, semolina, signorina.

-ina (-ī-), china, China, Dinah, Heine, Ina, myna; Regina; Carolina.

-inal, binal, crinal, final, spinal, trinal, vinyl; acclinal, caninal, equinal, piscinal; anticlinal, officinal, semifinal.

-inas. See **-inus.**

-inca, Inca, Katrinka.

-incher, clincher, flincher, lyncher, pincher.

-inctly, distinctly, succinctly; indistinctly.

-incture, cincture, tincture; encincture.

-inder, cinder, flinder, tinder; rescinder.

-indle, brindle, dwindle, kindle, spindle, swindle; enkindle, rekindle.

-indly, blindly, kindly; unkindly.

-indy, Hindi, Lindy, shindy, windy.

-inea. See **-inny.**

-inear. See **-innier.**

-inely, finely; benignly, caninely, divinely, supinely; saturninely.

-inement. See **-ignment.**

-iner, diner, finer, liner, miner, minor, shiner, Shriner, signer, winer; airliner, assigner, consignor, definer, designer, refiner; penny-a-liner.

-inet. See **-innet.**

-inew. See **-inue.**

-iney. See **-iny.**

-inful, sinful, skinful.

-ingent, stringent; astringent, constringent, contingent, restringent.

-inger (-ĭn-jər), cringer, fringer, ginger, hinger, injure, singer, twinger; infringer.

-inger (-ĭng-ər), bringer, flinger, ringer, singer, slinger, springer, stinger, stringer, wringer; humdinger; Meistersinger, minnesinger.

-inger (-ĭng-gər), finger, linger; malinger.

-ingle, cingle, cringle, dingle, ingle, jingle, mingle, shingle, single, swingle, tingle, tringle; commingle, Kris Kringle, surcingle; intermingle.

-ingly, jingly, mingly, shingly, singly, tingly.

-ingo, bingo, dingo, gringo, jingo, lingo, stingo; Domingo, flamingo.

-ingy (-ĭng-ē), clingy, dinghy, springy, stingy, stringy, swingy, wingy.

-ingy (-ĭn-jē), cringy, dingy, fringy, stingy, swingy, twingy.

-ini. See **-eeny.**

-inian. See **-inion.**

-inic, clinic, cynic, finic, quinic; actinic, aclinic, delphinic, fulminic, platinic, rabbinic; Jacobinic, narcotinic, nicotinic, polygynic.

-ining, dining, lining.
  Also: **-ine** + **-ing** (as in *mining*, etc.)
  Also: **-ign** + **-ing** (as in *signing*, etc.)

-inion, minion, pinion; Darwinian, dominion, opinion, Virginian; Abyssinian, Augustinian, Carolinian, Carthaginian, Palestinian.

-inish (-ĭn-), finish, Finnish, thinnish, tinnish; diminish.

-inish (-ī-), brinish, swinish.

-inist, plenist; machinist, routinist; magazinist.
  Also: **-ean** + **-est** (as in *cleanest*, etc.)
  Also: **-een** + **-est** (as in *greenest*, etc.)

-injure. See **-inger.**

-inker, blinker, clinker, drinker, inker, shrinker, sinker, slinker, stinker, thinker, tinker, winker.

-inkle, crinkle, inkle, sprinkle, tinkle, twinkle, winkle, wrinkle; besprinkle; periwinkle.

-inkling, inkling, sprinkling, tinkling, twinkling, wrinkling.

-inky, blinky, dinky, inky, kinky, pinky; Helsinki.

-inland, Finland, inland.

-inly, inly, thinly; McKinley.

-inner, dinner, finner, grinner, inner, pinner,

sinner, skinner, spinner, tinner, winner;
beginner, muleskinner.

-innet, ginnet, linnet, minute, spinet.

-innier, finnier, linear, skinnier.

-innish. See **-inish.**

-innow, minnow, winnow.

-inny, finny, guinea, Guinea, hinny, Minnie,
ninny, pinny, Pliny, skinny, spinney, tinny,
vinny, whinny, Winnie; Virginny; ignominy,
pickaninny.

-ino (-ī-), lino, rhino; albino.

-ino (-ē-). See **-eno.**

-inor. See **-iner.**

-inous. See **-inus.**

-inster, minster, Münster, spinster; Leominster,
Westminster.

-intel, lintel, pintle, quintal.

-inter, dinter, hinter, minter, printer, splinter,
sprinter, squinter, stinter, tinter, winter.

-into, pinto, Shinto.

-intry, splintery, vintry, wintry.

-inty, Dinty, flinty, glinty, linty, minty, squinty.

-inue, sinew; continue, retinue; discontinue.

-inus, binous, dryness, highness, linous, minus,
shyness, sinus, slyness, spinous, vinous;
Aquinas, echinus, lupinus, salinous, Your
Highness.

-inute. See **-innet.**

-iny (-ī-), briny, miny, piney, shiny, spiny, tiny,
twiny, viny, whiney, winy; sunshiny.

-iny (-ĭ-). See **-inny.**

-inyl. See **-inal.**

-io. See **-eo.**

-ion, Bryan, ion, lion, scion, Zion; anion, cation, O'Brien, Orion; dandelion.

-iot. See -iet.

-ious. See -ias.

-ipend, ripened, stipend.

-iper, diaper, griper, piper, riper, sniper, striper, swiper, typer, viper, wiper; bagpiper; windshield wiper.

-ipher. See -ifer.

-iple (-ī-), disciple, ectypal.

-iple (-ĭ-). See -ipple.

-iplet, liplet, triplet.

-ipling. See -ippling.

-ippe. See -ippy.

-ipper, chipper, clipper, dipper, flipper, gypper, kipper, nipper, shipper, sipper, skipper, slipper, snipper, stripper, tipper, tripper, whipper; Yom Kippur.

-ippet, sippet, skippet, snippet, tippet, whippet.

-ippi. See -ippy.

-ipple, cripple, nipple, ripple, stipple, tipple, triple.

-ippling, crippling, Kipling, rippling, stippling, tippling.

-ippo, hippo, Lippo.

-ippy, chippy, drippy, grippy, lippy, nippy, slippy, snippy, zippy; Xanthippe; Mississippi.

-ipsy. See -ypsy.

-iptic. See -yptic.

-iquant. See -ecant.

-iquely. See -eakly.

-iquor. See -icker.

-ira, Ira, Myra; Elmira, hegira, Palmyra.

-irant, gyrant, spirant, tyrant; aspirant, conspirant, expirant.

-irate. See **-yrate.**

-irchen, birchen, urchin.

-irder. See **-urder.**

-irdie. See **-urdy.**

-irdle, curdle, girdle, hurdle; engirdle.

-irdly, birdly, curdly, thirdly; absurdly.

-ireling, hireling, squireling.

-irely, direly; entirely.

-ireme, bireme, trireme.

-iren, Byron, siren; environ.

-iric. See **-yric.**

-irgin. See **-urgeon.**

-irgy. See **-urgy.**

-irker, burker, irker, jerker, lurker, shirker, smirker, worker.

-irler. See **-urler.**

-irling. See **-urling.**

-irlish, churlish, girlish.

-irly. See **-urly.**

-irma. See **-urma.**

-irmant. See **-erment.**

-irmer, firmer, murmur, squirmer, termer; affirmer, confirmer, infirmer.

-irmish, firmish, skirmish, squirmish, wormish.

-irmy. See **-ermy.**

-iro, Cairo, giro, gyro, tyro; autogiro.

-iron. See **-iren.**

-irous. See **-irus.**

-irrup, chirrup, stirrup, syrup.

-irter. See **-erter.**

-irtle. See **-urtle.**

-irty, Bertie, cherty, dirty, flirty, Gertie, shirty, spurty, squirty, thirty.

-irus, Cyrus, virus; desirous, papyrus.

-iry, briery, diary, fiery, friary, miry, priory, spiry, squiry, wiry; enquiry.

-isal, reprisal; paradisal.

-iscal, discal, fiscal.

-iscount, discount, miscount.

-iscuit. See -isket.

-iscus, discus, discous, viscous; hibiscus, meniscus.

-isel. See -izzle.

-isely, nicely; concisely, precisely.

-iser. See -isor.

-isher, disher, fisher, fissure, swisher, wisher; kingfisher, well-wisher.

-ishy, fishy, swishy.

-isian. See -ision.

-isic. See -ysic.

-ision, vision; collision, concision, decision, derision, division, elision, Elysian, envision, excision, incision, misprision, Parisian, precision, prevision, provision, recision, rescission, revision; circumcision, phonevision, stratovision, subdivision, supervision, television.

-isis, crisis, Isis, phthisis.

-isive, decisive, derisive, divisive, incisive; indecisive.

-isker, brisker, frisker, risker, whisker; bewhisker.

-isket, biscuit, brisket, tisket, trisket, wisket.

-isky, frisky, risky, whiskey.

-island, highland, island, Thailand.

-isly. See **-izzly.**

-ismal, dismal; abysmal, baptismal; cataclysmal, catechismal, paroxysmal.

-ison. See **-izen.**

-isor, geyser, Kaiser, miser, sizar, visor; adviser, divisor, incisor; supervisor.
    Also: **-ise** + **-er** (as in *reviser*, etc.)
    Also: **-ize** + **-er** (as in *sterilizer*, etc.)

-isper, crisper, lisper, whisper.

-ispy, crispy, lispy, wispy.

-issal. See **-istle.**

-issant. See **-ecent.**

-issile. See **-istle.**

-ission. See **-ition.**

-issor. See **-izzer.**

-issue, issue, tissue; reissue.

-issure. See **-isher.**

-ista, vista, Batista.

-istance, distance; assistance, consistence, desistance, existence, insistence, persistence, resistance, subsistence; coexistence, equidistance, nonexistence, nonresistance.

-istant, distant; assistant, consistent, existent, insistent, persistent, resistant, subsistent; coexistent, equidistant, inconsistent, nonexistent, nonresistant.

-isten, christen, glisten, listen.

-istence. See **-istance.**

-istent. See **-istant**

-ister, bister, blister, glister, mister, sister, twister; insister, persister, resister.

-istic, cystic, fistic, mystic; ballistic, deistic, juristic, linguistic, logistic, puristic, sadistic, simplistic, sophistic, statistic, stylistic, theistic, touristic; altruistic, anarchistic, animistic, atavistic, atheistic, bolshevistic, cabalistic, casuistic, catechistic, chauvinistic, communistic, egoistic, egotistic, euphuistic, fatalistic, humanistic, journalistic, nihilistic, optimistic, pantheistic, pessimistic, pietistic, pugilistic, realistic, socialistic, solecistic, syllogistic; anachronistic, capitalistic, characteristic, idealistic, polytheistic, rationalistic, ritualistic, sensualistic; materialistic, spiritualistic; individualistic.

-istine, Christine, pristine, Sistine; Philistine; amethystine.

-istle, bristle, fissile, gristle, istle, missal, missile, scissel, sissile, thistle, whistle; abyssal, dickcissel, dismissal, epistle.

-istmas, Christmas, isthmus.

-itain. See -itten.

-ital, title, vital; entitle, recital, requital, subtitle.

-itan. See -ighten.

-itcher, ditcher, hitcher, itcher, pitcher, richer, stitcher, switcher.

-itchy, bitchy, hitchy, itchy, pitchy, twitchy.

-ite. See -ighty.

-iteful. See -ightful.

-itely. See -ightly.

-itement, excitement, incitement, indictment.

-iten. See -ighten.

-iter. See -ighter.

-itey. See -ighty.

-ither (-ī-), blither, either, lither, neither, tither, writher.

-ither (-ĭ-), blither, dither, hither, thither, slither, whither, wither.

-ithesome, blithesome, lithesome.

-ithing, scything, tithing, writhing.

-ithy, pithy, smithy.

-iti. See **-eaty.**

-itial. See **-icial.**

-itic, critic; arthritic, dendritic, Hamitic, Levitic, mephitic, proclitic, rachitic, Semitic; biolytic, catalytic, cenobitic, eremitic, hypocritic, Jesuitic, paralytic, syphillitic.

-iting, biting, whiting; handwriting.
Also: **-ight** + **-ing** (as in *fighting*, etc.)
Also: **-ite** + **-ing** (as in *uniting*, etc.)
Also: **-ict** + **-ing** (as in *indicting*, etc.)

-ition, fission, mission; addition, admission, ambition, attrition, audition, cognition, coition, commission, condition, contrition, dentition, edition, emission, fruition, Galician, ignition, logician, magician, monition, munition, musician, nutrition, omission, optician, partition, patrician, perdition, permission, petition, physician, position, remission, rendition, sedition, submission, suspicion, tactician, tradition, transition, transmission, tuition, volition; abolition, acquisition, admonition, ammunition, apparition, apposition, coalition, competition, composition, definition, demolition, deposition, disposition, disquisition, ebullition, electrician, erudition, exhibition, expedition, exposition, extradition, imposition, inanition, inhibition, intermission, intuition, manumission, obstetrician, opposition, parturition, politician, premonition, preposition, prohibition, proposition, recognition, repetition, requisition, rhetorician, statistician, superstition, supposition, transposition; academician, arithmetician, decomposition, dialectician, geometrician, indisposition, inquisition; interposition, juxtaposition, mathematician, metaphysician, predisposition, presupposition.

-itious. See **-icious.**

-itish, British, skittish.

-itle. See **-ital.**

-itness, fitness, witness.

-iton (-ī-). See **-ighten.**

-iton (-ĭ-). See **-itten.**

-itsy. See **-itzy.**

-ittal. See **-ittle.**

-ittance, pittance, quittance; admittance, remittance.

-ittee. See **-itty.**

-itten, bitten, Britain, Briton, kitten, mitten, smitten, witan, written.

-itter, bitter, fitter, flitter, fritter, glitter, hitter, jitter, knitter, litter, pitter, quitter, sitter, spitter, splitter, titter, twitter; atwitter, committer, embitter, transmitter; baby-sitter, counterfeiter.

-itti. See **-itty.**

-ittle, brittle, knittle, little, skittle, spittle, tittle, victual, whittle; acquittal, belittle, committal, lickspittle, remittal, transmittal.

-ittler, Hitler, victualler, whittler; belittler.

-itty, city, ditty, flitty, gritty, kitty, Kitty, nitty, pity, pretty, witty; banditti, committee.

-itual, ritual; habitual.

-ity. See **-itty.**

-itzy, Fritzy, Mitzi, Ritzy; itsy bitsy.

-ival, rival; archival, arrival, revival, survival; adjectival, conjunctival; imperatival, nominatival.

-ivance, connivance, contrivance, survivance.

-ivel, civil, drivel, shrivel, snivel, swivel; uncivil.

-iven, driven, given, riven, scriven, shriven; forgiven.

-iver (-ĭv-), flivver, giver, liver, quiver, river, shiver, sliver; deliver, forgiver.

-iver (-ī-), diver, driver, fiver, hiver, Ivor, liver, shriver, skiver; conniver, contriver, deriver, reviver, survivor.

-ivet, civet, pivot, divot, privet, rivet, trivet.

-ivid, livid, vivid.

-ivil. See **-ivel.**

-ivor. See **-iver.**

-ivot. See **-ivet.**

-ivver. See **-iver.**

-ivvy. See **-ivy.**

-ivy, civvy, divvy, Livy, privy, skivvy, skivy, tivy; tantivy.

-ixer, fixer, mixer; elixir.

-ixie, Dixie, nixie, pixie, tricksy.

-ixture, fixture, mixture; admixture, commixture, immixture; intermixture.

-izard. See **-izzard.**

-izen (-ĭ-), dizen; bedizen, horizon.

-izen (-ī-), dizen, mizzen, prison, wizen; arisen, bedizen, imprison.

-izier. See **-izzier.**

-izzard, blizzard, gizzard, izzard, lizard, scissored, vizard, wizard.

-izzer, quizzer, scissor, whizzer.

-izzier, busier, dizzier, frizzier, vizier.

-izzle, chisel, drizzle, fizzle, frizzle, grizzle, mizzle, sizzle, swizzle.

-izzly, drizzly, frizzly, grisly, grizzly, sizzly.

-izzy, busy, dizzy, frizzy, Lizzie, tizzy.

-oa, boa, Goa, moa, Noah, proa; aloha, Genoa, jerboa, Samoa; protozoa.

-oader, goader, loader, odor; breechloader, corroder, exploder, foreboder, malodor; muzzleloader.

-oafy, loafy, oafy, Sophie, strophe, trophy.

-oaken. See **-oken.**

-oaker. See **-oker.**

-oaky. See **-oky.**

-oaler. See **-oller.**

-oaly. See **-oly.**

-oamer. See **-omer.**

-oaner. See **-oner.**

-oarder. See **-order.**

-oarer. See **-orer.**

-oarish, boarish, whorish.

-oarsely, coarsely, hoarsely.

-oary. See **-ory.**

-oastal, coastal, postal.

-oaster, boaster, coaster, poster, roaster, toaster; bill-poster, four-poster.

-oaten, oaten; verboten.

-oater. See **-otor.**

-oatswain. See **-osen.**

-oaty, floaty, goatee, oaty, throaty, zloty; coyote; Don Quixote.

-obate, globate, probate.

-obber, blobber, clobber, cobber, jobber, lobber, robber, slobber, sobber, swabber, throbber.

-obbin, bobbin, Dobbin, robbin, robin, Robin.

-obble, cobble, gobble, hobble, nobble, squabble, wobble.

-obbler, cobbler, gobbler, squabbler, wobbler.

-obby, bobby, Bobby, cobby, hobby, knobby, lobby, mobby, Robbie, snobby.

-obe, obi, Gobi; adobe.

-ober, prober, sober; disrober, October.

-obin. See **-obbin.**

-obo, hobo, lobo, oboe.

-obster, lobster, mobster.

-ocal, bocal, focal, local, phocal, vocal, yokel; bifocal.

-occer. See **-ocker.**

-ocean. See **-otion.**

-ocer, closer, grocer, grosser; engrosser, jocoser, moroser.

-ochee. See **-oky.**

-ocher. See **-oker.**

-ocile. See **-ostle.**

-ocker, blocker, clocker, cocker, docker, Fokker, knocker, locker, mocker, rocker, shocker, soccer, socker, stocker; knickerbocker.

-ockey. See **-ocky.**

-ocious, atrocious, ferocious, precocious.

-ocket, brocket, Crockett, docket, locket, pocket, rocket, socket, sprocket; pickpocket, vest-pocket.

-ocky, cocky, crocky, flocky, hockey, jockey, locky, rocky, sake, Saki, stocky; sukiyaki.

-oco, boko, coco, cocoa, loco; baroco, rococo; locofoco, Orinoco.

-ocoa. See **-oco.**

-ocre. See **-oker.**

-octer. See **-octor.**

-oction, concoction, decoction.

-octor, doctor, proctor; concocter, decocter.

-ocus, crocus, focus, hocus, locus; Hohokus; hocus-pocus.

-ocust, focused, locust.

-oda, coda, Rhoda, soda; Baroda, pagoda.

-odal, modal, nodal, yodel.

-odden, hodden, sodden, trodden; downtrodden, untrodden.

-odder, codder, dodder, fodder, nodder, odder, plodder, prodder, solder.

-oddess, bodice, goddess.

-odding, codding, nodding, plodding, podding, prodding, wadding.

-oddle, coddle, model, noddle, swaddle, toddle, twaddle, waddle; remodel; mollycoddle.

-oddy. See **-ody.**

-odel (-ŏ-). See **-oddle.**

-odel (-ō-). See **-odal.**

-oder. See **-oader.**

-odest, bodiced, modest, oddest; immodest.

-odger, codger, dodger, Dodger, lodger, Roger.

-odic, odic; anodic, iodic, melodic, methodic, rhapsodic, spasmodic, synodic; episodic, periodic.

-odice. See **-oddess.**

-odling, coddling, codling, godling, modeling, swaddling, toddling, twaddling, waddling.

-odly, godly, oddly; ungodly.

-odo, dodo; Quasimodo.

-odor. See **-oader.**

-odule, module, nodule.

-ody, body, cloddy, Mahdi, noddy, Roddy, shoddy, soddy, toddy, wadi; embody, nobody, somebody; anybody, busybody, everybody.

-oeia. See **-ea.**

-oem, poem, proem.

-oeman. See **-omen.**

-oer. See **-ower.**

-offal, offal, waffle.

-offee, coffee, toffee.

-offer, coffer, cougher, doffer, goffer, offer, proffer, scoffer.

-offin. See **-often.**

-offing, coughing, doffing, offing, scoffing.

-often, coffin, dauphin, often, soften.

-ofty, lofty, softy.

-oga, toga, yoga; Saratoga; Ticonderoga.

-ogan, brogan, hogan, Hogan, slogan.

-oger. See **-odger.**

-ogey. See **-ogie.**

-oggish, doggish, froggish, hoggish

-oggle, boggle, coggle, goggle, joggle, toggle; boondoggle, hornswoggle.

-oggy, boggy, cloggy, doggy, foggy, froggy, groggy, joggy, soggy.

-ogi. See **-ogie.**

-ogie, bogey, bogie, dogie, fogey, stogie, Yogi.

-ogle, bogle, ogle.

-oic, stoic; azoic, benzoic, dyspnoic, heroic; Cenozoic, Eozoic, Mesozoic, unheroic, protozoic; Paleozoic.

-oidal, colloidal, spheroidal.

-oider, voider; avoider, embroider.

-oily, coyly, doily, oily, roily.

-oiner, coiner; enjoiner, purloiner.

-ointer, jointer, pointer; anointer.

-ointment, ointment; anointment, appointment, disjointment; disappointment.

-oister, cloister, foister, hoister, moister, oyster, roister; Roister-Doister.

-oiter, goiter, loiter; exploiter, reconnoiter.

-oity, dacoity; hoity-toity.

-okay, croquet, okay, Tokay.

-okel. See **-ocal.**

-oken, broken, oaken, spoken, token; bespoken, betoken, foretoken, heartbroken, Hoboken, outspoken, unbroken, unspoken.

-oker, broker, choker, cloaker, croaker, joker, ocher, poker, soaker, smoker, stoker, stroker, yoker; convoker, evoker, invoker, provoker, revoker, stockbroker; mediocre.

-okey. See **-oky.**

-okum, hokum, locum, oakum.

-oky, choky, croaky, hokey, jokey, oaky, poky, soaky, smoky, troche, trochee; hoky-poky, okey-dokey.

-ola, cola, kola, Lola, Nola, Zola; Angola, gondola, Mazola, viola; Coca-Cola, Gorgonzola, Pensacola, Pepsi-Cola.

-olar (-ŏ-). See **-ollar.**

-olar (-ō-). See **-oller.**

-olden, golden, olden; beholden, embolden.

-older (-ōl-), bolder, boulder, colder, folder, holder, molder, moulder, older, shoulder, smolder; beholder, householder, upholder.

-older (-ŏd-). See **-odder.**

-oldly, boldly, coldly.

-oleful, bowlful, doleful, soulful.

-olely. See **-oly.**

-olemn. See **-olumn.**

-olen. See **-olon.**

-oler (-ŏ-). See **-ollar.**

-oler (-ō-). See **-oller.**

-olic, colic, frolic, rollick; bucolic, carbolic, embolic, symbolic, systolic; alcoholic, apostolic, diastolic, diabolic, epistolic, hyperbolic, melancholic, metabolic, parabolic, vitriolic.

-olid, solid, squalid, stolid.

-olish, polish; abolish, demolish.

-ollar, choler, collar, dollar, loller, scholar, squalor.

-ollard, bollard, Lollard, pollard.

-ollege. See **-owledge.**

-ollen. See **-olon.**

-oller, bowler, coaler, doler, droller, molar, polar, poller, roller, solar, stroller, toller, troller; cajoler, comptroller, consoler, controller, enroller, extoller, patroller; Holy Roller.

-ollick. See **-olic.**

-ollie. See **-olly.**

-ollins, Collins, Hollins, Rollins.

-ollo. See **-ollow.**

-ollop, dollop, lollop, scallop, trollop, wallop.

-ollow, follow, hollo, hollow, Rollo, swallow, wallow; Apollo.

-olly (-ŏ-), Bali, collie, Dollie, dolly, folly, golly, holly, jolly, Molly, polly, Polly, trolley, volley; finale, loblolly, tamale; melancholy.

-olly (-ō-). See -oly.

-olo, bolo, polo, solo.

-olon, colon, solon, Solon, stolen, swollen; semicolon.

-olonel. See -ernal.

-olor. See -uller.

-olster, bolster, holster; upholster.

-olter, bolter, colter, jolter, poulter; revolter.

-oltish, coltish, doltish.

-olumn, column, solemn.

-olver, solver; absolver, dissolver, evolver, resolver, revolver.

-oly (-ō-), coaly, drolly, goalie, holy, lowly, moly, shoaly, solely, slowly, wholly; Stromboli; roly-poly.

-oly (-ŏ-). See -olly.

-oma, coma, Roma, soma; aboma, aroma, diploma, Natoma, sarcoma, Tacoma; carcinoma, la paloma.

-omach, hummock, stomach.

-omain, domain, ptomaine, romaine.

-oman. See -omen.

-ombat, combat, wombat.

-omber. See -omer.

-ombie, Dombey, zombie; Abercrombie.

-omely. See -umbly.

-omen, bowman, foeman, gnomon, omen, Roman, showman, yeoman; abdomen, cognomen.

-oment, foment, moment; bestowment.

-omer (-ō-), comber, homer, Homer, omer, roamer; beachcomber, misnomer.

-omer (-ŭ-). See **-ummer**.

-omet, comet, grommet, vomit; Mahomet.

-omic, comic, gnomic; atomic; agronomic, anatomic, astronomic, autonomic, diatomic, economic, monatomic, taxonomic.

-omit. See **-omet**.

-omma. See **-ama**.

-ommy. See **-almy**.

-omo, chromo, Como, homo; major-domo.

-ompass, compass, rumpus; encompass.

-ompter, compter, prompter; accompter.

-onal, tonal, zonal.

-onday. See **-undy**.

-ondent, fondant, frondent; despondent, respondent; co-respondent, correspondent.

-onder, blonder, bonder, condor, fonder, ponder, squander, wander, yonder; absconder, desponder, responder; corresponder.

-one. See **-ony**.

-onely. See **-only**.

-onent, sonant; component, deponent, exponent, opponent, proponent.

-oner, boner, donor, droner, groaner, loaner, loner, moaner, owner, phoner; atoner, condoner, intoner.

-onest, honest, non est, wannest; dishonest.

-oney (-ō-). See **-ony**.

-oney (-ŭ-). See **-unny**.

-onger (-ŏ-), conger, longer, stronger, wronger; prolonger.

-onger (-ŭ-). See **-unger**.

-onging, longing, thronging, wronging; belonging, prolonging.

-ongly, strongly, wrongly.

-ongo, bongo, Congo.

-oni. See **-ony.**

-onic, chronic, conic, phonic, sonic, tonic; agonic, bubonic, Byronic, canonic, carbonic, colonic, cyclonic, demonic, draconic, euphonic, harmonic, hedonic, ionic, ironic, laconic, masonic, mnemonic, platonic, sardonic, Slavonic, symphonic, tectonic, Teutonic; diaphonic, diatonic, embryonic, histrionic, Housatonic, hydroponic, isotonic, macaronic, monophonic, philharmonic, telephonic; architectonic.

-onion, bunion, Bunyan, onion, Runyon, trunnion.

-onish, donnish, wannish; admonish, astonish, premonish.

-onkey. See **-unky.**

-only, lonely, only.

-onnet, bonnet, sonnet.

-onnie, Bonnie, bonny, Connie, Johnny, Lonny, Ronnie.

-onor (-ŏ-), goner, honor, wanner; dishonor.

-onor (-ō-). See **-oner.**

-onsil, consul, tonsil; proconsul, responsal.

-onsul. See **-onsil.**

-ontal. See **-untle.**

-onter. See **-unter.**

-ontract, contract, entr' acte.

-onus, bonus, Honus, onus.

-ony, bony, Coney, cony, crony, drony, phony, pony, stony, tony, Tony; baloney, Marconi,

Shoshone, spumoni, tortoni; abalone, alimony, antimony, cicerone, lazzaroni, macaroni, matrimony, minestrone, parsimony, patrimony, sanctimony, testimony.

-ooby, booby, ruby, Ruby.

-oocher. See **-uture.**

-ooding, hooding, pudding.

-oodle, boodle, doodle, feudal, noodle, strudel; caboodle, flapdoodle, kiyoodle; Yankee Doodle.

-oody (-ŏŏ-), goody, woody.

-oody (-ōō-), broody, Judy, moody.

-oody (-ŭ-). See **-uddy.**

-ooey. See **-ewy.**

-ookie. See **-ooky.**

-ookish, bookish, rookish, spookish.

-ooky (-ŏŏ-), bookie, cooky, hookey, hooky, rookie.

-ooky (-ōō-), fluky, spooky; Kabuki.

-oolie. See **-uly.**

-oolish, coolish, foolish, mulish.

-oolly (-ŏŏ-). See **-ully.**

-oolly (-ōō-). See **-uly.**

-oomer. See **-umer.**

-oomy, bloomy, gloomy, plumy, rheumy, roomy.

-ooner. See **-uner.**

-oony, loony, moony, spoony.

-ooper, blooper, cooper, grouper, hooper, snooper, stupor, super, trooper, whooper; superduper.

-oopy, croupy, droopy, rupee, soupy, whoopee.

-oorish, boorish, Moorish.

-ooser. See **-oser.**

-oosy (-ōō zĭ). See **-oozy.**

-oosy (-ōō sĭ). See **-uicy.**

-ooter, cuter, hooter, looter, mooter, neuter, pewter, rooter, scooter, tutor; commuter, computer, disputer, freebooter, polluter, refuter.

-oothless. See **-uthless.**

-ootie. See **-ooty.**

-ooty, beauty, booty, cootie, cutie, duty, fluty, fruity, rooty, snooty, sooty; agouti.

-ooza. See **-usa.**

-oozer. See **-oser.**

-oozle, foozle, fusel, ousel; bamboozle, perusal, refusal.

-oozy, boozy, floosie, newsy, oozy, woosy.

-opal, opal, cpoal; Adrianople, Constantinople.

-oper (-ō-), groper, moper, roper, sloper, toper; eloper, interloper.

-oper (-ŏ-). See **-opper.**

-opey. See **-opy.**

-ophe. See **-oafy.**

-ophy. See **-oafy.**

-opic, topic, tropic; myopic; microscopic, misanthropic, philanthropic, presbyopic, spectroscopic, telescopic; heliotropic, kaleidoscopic, stereoscopic.

-ople. See **-opal.**

-opper, chopper, copper, cropper, hopper, popper, proper, shopper, stopper, topper, whopper; clodhopper, cornpopper, eavesdropper, grasshopper, improper, sharecropper, show-stopper.

-opping, chopping.

Also **-op** + **-ing** (as in *shopping*, etc.)

-opple, stoppel, topple; estoppel.

-oppy, choppy, copy, floppy, Hoppy, poppy, sloppy, soppy.

-opsy, copsy, dropsy, Topsy; autopsy, biopsy.

-opter, copter; adopter; helicopter.

-optic, coptic, optic; synoptic.

-option, option; adoption.

-opy (-ō-), dopey, Hopi, mopy, ropy, soapy.

-opy (-ŏ-). See **-oppy.**

-ora, aura, Cora, Dora, flora, Flora, hora, Laura, mora, Nora, Torah; Andorra, angora, Aurora, fedora, Marmora, menorah, Pandora, signora; Floradora.

-orage, borage, porridge, shorage, storage.

-oral, aural, chloral, choral, coral, floral, horal, laurel, moral, oral, quarrel, sorrel; auroral, immoral, sororal.

-orax, borax, corax, storax, thorax.

-orbel. See **-arble.**

-orchard, orchard, tortured.

-orcher, scorcher, torture.

-order, boarder, border, forder, hoarder, order, warder; disorder, recorder, rewarder.

-ordon, cordon, Gordon, Jordan, warden.

-ordship, lordship wardship.

-ordy. See **-urdy.**

-ore. See **-ory.**

-orehead. See **-orrid.**

-oreign, florin, foreign, warren.

-orer, borer, corer, horror, roarer, scorer, snorer; abhorrer, adorer, explorer, ignorer, restorer.

-oresail. See **-orsel.**

-orest, florist, forest, sorest.

-orey. See -ory.

-organ, gorgon, Morgan, organ.

-orger, forger, gorger, ordure; disgorger.

-ori. See -ory.

-oric, chloric, choric, Doric, Yorick; caloric, historic, phosphoric; allegoric, metaphoric, meteoric, paregoric, prehistoric, sophomoric.

-orid. See -orrid.

-oris, Boris, Doris, loris, Horace, Morris, Norris.

-orker. See -irker.

-ormal, formal, normal; abnormal, informal, subnormal.

-orman, doorman, floorman, foreman, Mormon, Norman; longshoreman.

-ormant, dormant; conformant, informant.

-ormer, dormer, former, stormer, warmer; barnstormer, conformer, informer, performer, reformer, transformer.

-ormish. See -irmish.

-ormy. See -ermy.

-orner, corner, horner, mourner, scorner, warner; adorner, suborner.

-ornet, cornet, hornet.

-orney. See -ourney.

-ornful, mournful, scornful.

-orning, morning, mourning, scorning, warning; adorning, forewarning.

-orny, corny, horny, thorny.

-orough, borough, burro, burrow, furrow, thorough.

-orous, chorus, porous, Taurus, torous, torus; decorous, imporous, pylorus, sonorous; ichthyosaurus.

-orpor, torpor, warper.

-orpus, corpus, porpoise.

-orrel. See **-oral.**

-orrent, torrent, warrant; abhorrent.

-orrid, florid, forehead, horrid, torrid.

-orridge. See **-orage.**

-orris. See **-oris.**

-orror. See **-orer.**

-orrow, borrow, morrow, sorrow; tomorrow.

-orry (-ŏ-), quarry, sorry. See also **-arry** and **-ory.**

-orry (-û-). See **-urry.**

-orsel, dorsal, foresail, morsel.

-orsen. See **-erson.**

-orsion. See **-ortion.**

-ortal, chortle, mortal, portal; immortal.

-orten, Horton, Morton, Norton, quartan, shorten.

-orter, mortar, porter, quarter, shorter, snorter, sorter; contorter, distorter, exporter, extorter, importer, reporter, ripsnorter, supporter.

-ortex, cortex, vortex.

-ortion, portion, torsion; abortion, apportion, consortion, contortion, distortion, extortion, proportion; disproportion.

-ortive, sportive, tortive; abortive, transportive.

-ortle. See **-ortal.**

-ortly, courtly, portly.

-ortment, assortment, comportment, deportment, disportment, transportment.

-orton. See **-orten.**

-ortune, fortune; importune, misfortune.

-orture. See **-orcher.**

-ortured. See **-orchard.**

-orty, forty, snorty, sortie, warty.

-orum, forum, quorum; decorum; ad valorem, indecorum, variorum.

-orus. See **-orous.**

-ory, dory, flory, glory, gory, hoary, lorry, storey, story, Tory; Old Glory, vainglory; allegory, a priori, category, con amore, desultory, dilatory, dormitory, gustatory, hortatory, hunky dory, inventory, laudatory, mandatory, migratory, offertory, oratory, peremptory, predatory, prefatory, promissory, promontory, purgatory, repertory, territory; a fortiori, cacciatore, circulatory, commendatory, compensatory, conciliatory, conservatory, declaratory, defamatory, depilatory, depository, deprecatory, derogatory, exclamatory, explanatory, inflammatory, laboratory, obligatory, observatory, preparatory, reformatory, respiratory, undulatory; a posteriori, retaliatory. See also **-orry.**

-osa, osa; Formosa, mimosa; Mariposa.

-osely, closely, grossly, jocosely, morosely, verbosely.

-osen, chosen, frozen, boatswain, hosen, squozen.

-oser (-o͞o zər), boozer, bruiser, chooser, cruiser, loser. See also **-user.**

-oser (-ō sər). See **-ocer.**

-oset. See **-osit.**

-osher, josher, washer.

-oshy, boshy, sloshy, squashy, swashy, toshy, washy.

-osier, crosier, hosier, osier.

-osion, ambrosian, corrosion, erosion, explosion, implosion.

-osit, closet, posit; deposit; juxtaposit.

-osive, corrosive, erosive, explosive.

-oso. See **-uso.**

-ossal. See **-ostle.**

-osser. See **-ocer.**

-ossil. See **-ostle.**

-ossom, blossom, possum; opossum.

-ossum. See **-ossom.**

-ossy, bossy, drossy, Flossie, flossy, glossy, mossy, posse, quasi, tossy.

-ostal, costal, hostel, hostile; infracostal, intercostal, Pentecostal.

-oster (-ŏ-), coster, foster, Gloucester, roster; accoster, imposter; paternoster, Pentecoster.

-oster (-ō-). See **-oaster.**

-ostic, caustic, gnostic; acrostic, agnostic, prognostic; anacrostic, diagnostic, paracrostic, pentacostic.

-ostle, docile, dossil, fossil, jostle, throstle, wassail; apostle, colossal.

-ostler, hostler, jostler, ostler, wassailer.

-ostly, ghostly, mostly.

-ostril, costrel, nostril, rostral.

-ostrum, nostrum, rostrum.

-osure, closure; composure, disclosure, enclosure, exposure, foreclosure, reposure; discomposure.

-osy, cosy, dozy, nosy, posy, prosy, Rosie, rosy.

-ota, quota, rota; Dakota, iota; Minnesota.

-otal, dotal, notal, rotal, total; sclerotal, teetotal; anecdotal, antidotal, extradotal, sacerdotal.

-otcher, blotcher, botcher, notcher, splotcher, watcher; topnotcher.

-otchy, blotchy, botchy, splotchy; Pagliacci; Liberace.

-ote. See -oaty.

-otem, totem; factotum.

-oter. See -otor.

-other (-ŏ-), bother, father, fother, pother.

-other (-ŭ-), brother, mother, other, smother; another.

-othing, clothing, loathing.

-othy, frothy, mothy.

-otic, chaotic, demotic, despotic, erotic, exotic, hypnotic, neurotic, narcotic, osmotic, pyrotic, quixotic, zymotic; idiotic, patriotic.

-otion, Goshen, lotion, motion, notion, ocean, potion; commotion, devotion, emotion, promotion, remotion; locomotion.

-otive, motive, votive; emotive, promotive; locomotive.

-otly, hotly, motley, squatly.

-oto, otoe, photo, toto; De Soto, Kyoto.

-otor, boater, bloater, doter, floater, motor, quoter, rotor, voter; promoter, pulmotor; locomotor.

-ottage, cottage, pottage, wattage.

-ottar. See -otter.

-otten, cotton, gotten, Groton, rotten; begotten, forgotten; misbegotten.

-otter, blotter, clotter, cottar, cotter, dotter, hotter, jotter, knotter, ottar, otter, plotter, potter, rotter, squatter, spotter, swatter, totter, trotter; complotter.

-ottish, schottische, Scottish, sottish.

-ottle, bottle, dottle, glottal, mottle, pottle, throttle, tottle, twattle, wattle.

-otto, blotto, grotto, lotto, motto, Otto, Watteau. See also **-ato (-ä-).**

-otton. See **-otten.**

-otty, blotty, clotty, dotty, knotty, Lottie, potty, snotty, spotty.

-ouble, bubble, double, rubble, stubble, trouble.

-oubly. See **-ubbly.**

-oubter. See **-outer.**

-oucher, croucher, Goucher, sloucher, voucher.

-ouder. See **-owder.**

-oudly, loudly, proudly.

-oudy. See **-owdy.**

-oughen, roughen, toughen.

-ougher (-ŏ-). See **-offer.**

-ougher (-ŭ-). See **-uffer.**

-oughly. See **-uffly.**

-oughty. See **-outy.**

-oulder. See **-older.**

-oulful. See **-oleful.**

-ouncil, council, counsel, groundsel.

-ounder, bounder, flounder, founder, hounder, pounder, rounder, sounder; confounder, expounder, propounder.

-oundly, roundly, soundly; profoundly, unsoundly.

-ounger. See **-unger.**

-ountain, fountain, mountain.

-ounter, counter, mounter; accounter, discounter, encounter, surmounter.

-ounty, bounty, county, mounty.

-ourage, courage; demurrage, discourage, encourage.

-ouper. See **-ooper.**

-ouple, couple, supple.

-oupy. See **-oopy.**

-ouri. See **-ury.**

-ourish, currish, flourish, nourish.

-ourist. See **-urist.**

-ourly, hourly, sourly.

-ourney, Ernie, journey, tourney; attorney.

-ournful. See **-ornful.**

-ourning. See **-orning.**

-ousal, housel, ousel, spousal, tousle; arousal, carousal, espousal.

-ousel. See **-ousal.**

-ouser, Bowser, browser, dowser, houser, Mauser, mouser, rouser, schnauzer, Towser, trouser; carouser.

-ousin. See **-ozen.**

-ousle. See **-ousal.**

-ousseau. See **-uso.**

-ousy, blowsy, drowsy, frowsy, lousy, mousy.

-outer, clouter, doubter, flouter, pouter, router, scouter, shouter, stouter, touter.

-outhful. See **-uthful.**

-outy, doughty, droughty, gouty, grouty, snouty.

-ova, nova; ova, Jehovah; Casanova, Villanova; Vita nuova.

-oval, approval, disproval, removal, reproval; disapproval.

-ovel, grovel, hovel, novel.

-ovement, movement; approvement, improvement.

-oven (-ō-), cloven, woven; interwoven.

-oven (-ŭ-), covin, oven, sloven.

-over (-ō-), clover, Dover, drover, over, plover, rover, stover, trover; moreover, pushover.

-over (-ŭ-), cover, lover, plover, shover; discover, recover, uncover.

-oward, coward, cowered, flowered, Howard, powered, showered, towered.

-owboy, cowboy, ploughboy.

-owder, chowder, crowder, louder, powder, prouder.

-owdy, cloudy, dowdy, howdy, rowdy; pandowdy.

-owel, bowel, dowel, rowel, towel, trowel, vowel; avowal; disembowel.

-ower, blower, crower, goer, grower, knower, lower, mower, ower, rower, sewer, slower, sower, thrower, tower; bestower; overthrower.

-owered. See -oward.

-owery, bowery, cowry, dowry, flowery, houri, showery, towery.

-owing, blowing, crowing, flowing, glowing, going, growing, knowing, lowing, mowing, owing, rowing, sewing, showing, snowing, sowing, stowing, towing, throwing.

Also: -ow + -ing (as in *bestowing*, etc.)

Also: -o + -ing (as in *outgoing*, etc.)

-owledge, college, knowledge; acknowledge, foreknowledge.

-owler. See -oller.

-owly. See -oly.

-owman. See -omen.

-owner. See -oner.

-ownie. See -owny.

-ownsman, gownsman, townsman.

-owny, brownie, Brownie, downy, frowny, towny.

-owry. See **-owery.**

-owsy. See **-ousy.**

-owy, blowy, Bowie, Chloë, doughy, glowy, Joey, showy, snowy.

-oxen, coxswain, oxen.

-oxy, Coxey, doxy, foxy, proxy; Biloxi; orthodoxy, paradoxy; heterodoxy.

-oyal, loyal, royal; disloyal.

-oyalty, loyalty, royalty.

-oyant, buoyant, clairvoyant, flamboyant.

-oyer, annoyer, destroyer, employer, enjoyer.

-oyish, boyish, coyish.

-oyly. See **-oily.**

-oyment, deployment, employment, enjoyment; unemployment.

-oyster. See **-oister.**

-ozen (-ŭ-), cousin, cozen, dozen.

-ozen (-ō-). See **-osen.**

-ozzle, nozzle, schnozzle.

-uager. See **-ager.**

-ual. See **-uel.**

-uant, fluent, truant; pursuant.

-uba, Cuba, juba, tuba.

-ubbard. See **-upboard.**

-ubber, blubber, clubber, drubber, dubber, grubber, lubber, rubber, scrubber, snubber, stubber; landlubber; money-grubber; india rubber.

-ubberd. See **-upboard.**

-ubbish, clubbish, cubbish, grubbish, rubbish, tubbish.

-ubble. See **-ouble.**

-ubbly, bubbly, doubly, knubbly, rubbly, stubbly.

-ubby, chubby, cubby, grubby, hubby, nubby, scrubby, shrubby, stubby, tubby.

-ubic, cubic, pubic, cherubic.

-ubtle. See **-uttle.**

-ubtler. See **-utler.**

-uby. See **-ooby.**

-ucent, lucent; abducent, adducent, traducent, translucent.

-ucial, crucial; fiducial.

-ucid, deuced, lucid, mucid; pellucid.

-ucker, bucker, chukker, mucker, pucker, succor, sucker, trucker, tucker; seersucker.

-uckett, bucket, tucket; Nantucket, Pawtucket.

-uckle, buckle, chuckle, huckle, knuckle, muckle, suckle, truckle; unbuckle; honeysuckle.

-uckled. See **-uckold.**

-uckler, buckler, chuckler, knuckler; swashbuckler.

-uckling, buckling, duckling, suckling.

-uckold, cuckold.

    Also: **-uckle** + **-d** (as in *buckled*, etc.)

-ucky, ducky, lucky, mucky, plucky; Kentucky, unlucky.

-ucre. See **-uker.**

-ucter. See **-uctor.**

-uction, fluxion, ruction, suction; abduction, adduction, affluxion, conduction, construction, deduction, defluxion, destruction, effluxion, induction, influxion, instruction, production, reduction, seduction, traduction;

introduction, reproduction, misconstruction; overproduction, superinduction.

-uctive, adductive, conductive, constructive, deductive, destructive, inductive, instructive, obstructive, productive, reductive, seductive, traductive; introductive, reproductive, superstructive; overproductive.

-uctor, ductor; abductor, adductor, conductor, constructor, destructor, eductor, instructor, obstructer; nonconductor.

-udder, dudder, flooder, mudder, rudder, scudder, shudder, udder.

-uddhist. See -udist.

-uddle, cuddle, huddle, muddle, puddle, ruddle.

-uddler, cuddler, huddler, muddler.

-uddy, bloody, buddy, cruddy, muddy, ruddy, studdy, study.

-udel. See -oodle.

-udely, crudely, lewdly, nudely, rudely, shrewdly.

-udent, prudent, student; concludent, imprudent; jurisprudent.

-udest. See -udist.

-udgeon, bludgeon, dudgeon, gudgeon; curmudgeon.

-udgy, pudgy, smudgy.

-udish, crudish, dudish, lewdish, nudish, prudish, rudish, shrewdish.

-udist, Buddhist, crudest, feudist, lewdest, nudist, rudest, shrewdest.

-udo, judo, pseudo; escudo, testudo.

-udy. See -uddy.

-uel, crewel, cruel, dual, duel, fuel, gruel, jewel,

newel; bejewel, eschewal, pursual, renewal, reviewal, subdual.

-uet, cruet, suet.

-uey. See **-ewy.**

-uffel. See **-uffle.**

-uffer, bluffer, buffer, duffer, gruffer, huffer, puffer, rougher, snuffer, stuffer, suffer, tougher.

-uffin, muffin, puffin; ragamuffin.

-uffing, bluffing, cuffing, huffing, puffing, stuffing.

-uffle, buffle, duffel, muffle, ruffle, scuffle, shuffle, snuffle, truffle.

-uffly, bluffly, gruffly, roughly, ruffly, shuffly, snuffly, toughly.

-uffy, fluffy, huffy, puffy, snuffy, stuffy.

-ufty, mufti, tufty.

-ugal. See **-ugle.**

-ugger, bugger, drugger, hugger, lugger, plugger, rugger, smugger, snugger, tugger; hugger-mugger.

-uggle, juggle, smuggle, snuggle, struggle.

-uggy, buggy, muggy, puggy, sluggy.

-ugle, bugle, frugal, fugal; MacDougall.

-ugly, smugly, snuggly, snugly, ugly.

-uicy, goosy, juicy, Lucy, sluicy; Debussy, Watusi.

-uid, druid, fluid.

-uilder, builder, gilder, guilder; bewilder, rebuilder.

-uilding, building, gilding; rebuilding.

-uin, bruin, ruin.

-uiser. See **-oser.**

-uitor. See **-ooter.**

-uker, euchre, fluker, lucre, puker; rebuker.

-uki. See **-ooky.**

-uky. See **-ooky.**

-ula, Beulah, hula; Talullah; Ashtabula, Boola Boola, hula-hula.

-ulep. See **-ulip.**

-ulgar, Bulgar, vulgar.

-ulgence, effulgence, indulgence, refulgence; self-indulgence.

-ulgent, fulgent; effulgent, indulgent, refulgent; self-indulgent.

-ulip, julep, tulip.

-ulky, bulky, hulky, sulky.

-uller, color, cruller, culler, duller, guller, luller, sculler; annuller, discolor, medullar, tricolor; Technicolor, multicolor, water color.

-ullet (-oo-), bullet, pullet.

-ullet (-ŭl-), cullet, gullet, mullet.

-ulley. See **-ully.**

-ullion, cullion, mullion, scullion.

-ully (-ool-), bully, fully, pulley, woolly.

-ully (-ŭl-), cully, dully, gully, hully, sully, Tully.

-ulsion, pulsion; compulsion, convulsion, divulsion, emulsion, expulsion, impulsion, propulsion, repulsion, revulsion.

-ulsive, compulsive, convulsive, divulsive, emulsive, expulsive, impulsive, propulsive, repulsive, revulsive.

-ultry, sultry; adultery.

-ulture, culture, vulture; agriculture, aviculture, floriculture, horticulture, pisciculture, viniculture.

-ulu, Lulu, Zulu; Honolulu.

-uly, coolie, coolly, Dooley, duly, Julie, newly, Thule, truly; unduly; Ultima Thule.

-uma, duma, puma, Yuma; mazuma; Montezuma.

-umage, fumage, plumage.

-uman. See -umen.

-umbent, accumbent, decumbent, incumbent, procumbent, recumbent.

-umber, cumber, Humber, lumbar, lumber, number, slumber, umber; cucumber, encumber, outnumber; disencumber.

-umber. See -ummer.

-umble, bumble, crumble, fumble, grumble, humble, jumble, mumble, rumble, scumble, stumble, tumble, umble.

-umbly, comely, dumbly, humbly, numbly.

-umbo, Dumbo, gumbo; mumbo-jumbo.

-umbrous, cumbrous, slumbrous; penumbrous.

-umby. See -ummy.

-umen, human, lumen, Truman; acumen, albumin, bitumen, illumine, inhuman, legumen; superhuman.

-umer, bloomer, boomer, fumer, humor, rumor, tumor; consumer, perfumer.

-umid, fumid, humid, tumid.

-umly. See -umbly.

-ummer, comer, drummer, dumber, hummer, mummer, number, plumber, scummer, summer; late-comer, midsummer, newcomer.

-ummit, plummet, summit.

-ummock. See -omach.

-ummy, crumby, crummy, dummy, gummy, lummy, mummy, plummy, rummy, scummy, thrummy, tummy, yummy.

-umnal, autumnal, columnal.

-umous, fumous, grumous, humous, humus, plumous, spumous, strumous.

-umper, bumper, dumper, jumper, plumper, pumper, stumper, trumper, thumper.

-umpet, crumpet, strumpet, trumpet.

-umpish, dumpish, frumpish, grumpish, lumpish, plumpish.

-umpkin, bumpkin, lumpkin, pumpkin.

-umple, crumple, rumple.

-umption, gumption; assumption, consumption, presumption, resumption.

-umptious, bumptious, scrumptious.

-umptive, assumptive, consumptive, presumptive, resumptive.

-umpus. See **-ompass.**

-umus. See **-umous.**

-una, luna, puna, Una; lacuna, vicuna.

-unar. See **-uner.**

-uncheon, bruncheon, luncheon, puncheon, truncheon.

-uncle, uncle; carbuncle.

-unction, function, junction, unction; compunction, conjunction, defunction, disjunction, expunction, injunction.

-unctive, adjunctive, conjunctive, disjunctive, subjunctive.

-uncture, juncture, puncture; conjuncture.

-undance, abundance, redundance; superabundance.

-undant, abundant, redundant; superabundant.

-unday. See **-undy.**

-under, blunder, sunder, thunder, under,

wonder; asunder, jocunder, refunder, rotunder, thereunder.

-undle, bundle, rundle, trundle.

-undy, Fundy, Grundy, Monday, Sunday, undie; salmagundi.

-uner, crooner, lunar, pruner, schooner, sooner, spooner, swooner, tuner; attuner, communer, harpooner, impugner, lacunar, oppugner; importuner.

-unger (-g-), hunger, monger, younger; fishmonger, gossipmonger, newsmonger; ironmonger.

-unger (-j-), blunger, lunger, plunger, sponger; expunger.

-ungle, bungle, jungle.

-unic, Munich, punic, Punic, runic, tunic.

-union. See **-onion.**

-unkard, bunkered, drunkard, Dunkard.

-unker, bunker, drunker, dunker, flunker, funker, junker, Junker, plunker, punker.

-unky, chunky, donkey, flunkey, funky, hunky, monkey, spunky.

-unnage. See **-onnage.**

-unnel, funnel, gunwale, runnel, tunnel.

-unny, bunny, funny, gunny, honey, money, sonny, sunny, Tunney, tunny.

-unster, funster, gunster, punster.

-untal. See **-untle.**

-unter, blunter, bunter, grunter, hunter, punter; confronter.

-untle, frontal, gruntle; disgruntle; contrapuntal.

-unwale. See **-unnel.**

-uoy. See **-ewy.**

-upboard, blubbered, cupboard, Hubbard, rubbered.

-uper. See **-ooper.**

-upil. See **-uple.**

-uple, pupil; scruple, octuple, quadruple, quintuple, septuple, sextuple.

-uplet, drupelet; octuplet, quadruplet, quintuplet, septuplet, sextuplet.

-upor. See **-ooper.**

-upper, crupper, scupper, supper, upper.

-upple. See **-ouple.**

-uppy, guppy, puppy.

-ura, pleura; bravura, caesura; Angostura; coloratura; appoggiatura.

-ural, crural, jural, mural, neural, pleural, plural, rural, Ural; intermural, intramural, sinecural.

-urance, durance; assurance, endurance, insurance; reassurance.

-urban, bourbon, Durban, turban, urban; suburban; interurban.

-urchin. See **-irchen.**

-urder, girder, herder, murder, sirdar; absurder, engirder, sheepherder.

-urdle. See **-irdle.**

-urdly. See **-irdly.**

-urdy, birdie, sturdy, Verdi, wordy; hurdygurdy.

-urely, purely; demurely, maturely, obscurely, securely.

-urement, abjurement, allurement, immurement, obscurement, procurement.

-urer, curer, führer, furor, juror, lurer, purer; abjuror, insurer, nonjuror, procurer, securer.

-urgate, expurgate, objurgate.

-urgence. See **-ergence.**

-urgent. See **-ergent.**

-urgeon, burgeon, sturgeon, surgeon, virgin.

-urger. See **-erger.**

-urgle, burgle, gurgle.

-urgy, clergy, dirgy, surgy; liturgy; dramaturgy, metallurgy, thaumaturgy.

-uric, purpuric, sulfuric, telluric.

-urist, jurist, purist, tourist; caricaturist.

-urker. See **-irker.**

-urky. See **-erky.**

-urler, burler, curler, furler, hurler, purler, skirler, twirler, whirler.

-urlew, curlew, purlieu.

-urling, curling, furling, hurling, purling, skirling, sterling, swirling, twirling, whirling; uncurling.

-urlish. See **-irlish.**

-urloin, purloin, sirloin.

-urly, burly, churly, curly, early, girlie, knurly, pearly, Shirley, surly, twirly, whirly; hurlyburly.

-urma, Burma, derma, Irma; terra firma.

-urmese. See **-ermes.**

-urmur. See **-irmer.**

-urnal. See **-ernal.**

-urner. See **-earner.**

-urning. See **-earning.**

-urnish, burnish, furnish.

-uror. See **-urer.**

-urper, burper, chirper; usurper.

-urrage. See **-ourage.**

-urrish. See **-ourish.**

-urro. See -orough.

-urrow. See -orough.

-urry, burry, curry, flurry, furry, hurry, scurry, slurry, surrey, worry.

-ursal. See -ersal.

-urser, bursar, cursor, mercer, nurser, purser; disburser, precursor.

-ursor. See -urser.

-urtain. See -ertain.

-urter. See -erter.

-urtive. See -ertive.

-urtle, fertile, hurtle, kirtle, myrtle, Myrtle, turtle, whirtle.

-urtly. See -ertly.

-urvant. See -ervant.

-urvy, curvy, nervy, scurvy; topsy-turvy.

-ury (-o͞o-), Curie, fury, houri, Jewry, jury; Missouri; potpourri.

-ury (-ĕ-). See -erry.

-usa, Sousa, Medusa; Arethusa; lallapalooza.

-usal. See -oozle.

-uscan, buskin, dusken, Ruskin, Tuscan; Etruscan, molluscan.

-uscle. See -ustle.

-usel. See -oozle.

-useless, useless; excuseless.

-user, user; abuser, accuser, amuser, diffuser, excuser. See also -oser.

-usher, blusher, brusher, crusher, flusher, gusher, husher, plusher, rusher, usher; four-flusher.

-ushy, gushy, mushy, plushy, slushy.

-usi. See -uicy.

-usier. See -izzier.

-usion, fusion; allusion, Carthusian, collusion, conclusion, confusion, contusion, delusion, diffusion, effusion, elusion, exclusion, extrusion, illusion, inclusion, infusion, intrusion, Malthusian, obtrusion, occlusion, profusion, protrusion, reclusion, seclusion, suffusion, transfusion; disillusion, interfusion.

-usive, abusive, allusive, collusive, conclusive, conducive, delusive, diffusive, effusive, exclusive, illusive, inclusive, infusive, intrusive, obtrusive, reclusive, seclusive; inconclusive.

-uskin, buskin, Ruskin.

-usky, dusky, husky, musky, tusky.

-uso, Crusoe, Rousseau, trousseau, whoso; Caruso.

-ussel. See **-ustle.**

-usset, gusset, russet.

-ussia, Prussia, Russia.

-ussian. See **-ussion.**

-ussion, Prussian, Russian; concussion, discussion, percussion; repercussion.

-ussive, concussive, discussive, percussive; repercussive.

-ussy, fussy, Gussie, hussy, mussy.

-ustard, blustered, bustard, clustered, custard, flustered, mustard, mustered.

-uster, bluster, buster, cluster, Custer, duster, fluster, juster, luster, muster, thruster, truster; adjuster, distruster, lackluster; coadjuster, filibuster.

-ustered. See **-ustard.**

-ustic, fustic, rustic.

-ustion, fustian; combustion.

-ustle, bustle, hustle, justle, muscle, mussel, rustle, tussle.

-ustler, bustler, hustler, rustler, tussler.

-ustly, justly; augustly, robustly, unjustly.

-usty, busty, dusty, gusty, lusty, musty, rusty, trusty.

-usy. See **-izzy.**

-utal, brutal, footle, tootle; refutal.

-uter. See **-ooter.**

-utest. See **-utist.**

-uthful, ruthful, truthful, youthful; untruthful.

-uthless, ruthless, toothless, truthless.

-utie. See **-ooty.**

-utile, futile; inutile.

-ution, ablution, dilution, locution, pollution, solution, volution; absolution, attribution, commination, constitution, contribution, convolution, destitution, devolution, diminution, dissolution, distribution, elocution, evolution, execution, institution, involution, Lilliputian, persecution, prosecution, prostitution, resolution, restitution, retribution, revolution, substitution; circumlocution, electrocution, irresolution.

-utist, cutest, flutist, lutist; pharmaceutist, therapeutist.

-utive, coadjutive, constitutive, diminutive, persecutive, resolutive.

-utor. See **-ooter.**

-uttal. See **-uttle.**

-utter, butter, clutter, cutter, flutter, gutter, mutter, putter, shutter, splutter, sputter, strutter, stutter, utter; abutter, rebutter, woodcutter.

-uttish, ruttish, sluttish.

-uttle, butle, cuttle, scuttle, shuttle, subtle; rebuttal.

-uttler. See **-utler.**

-utton, button, glutton, mutton; bachelor button.

-utty, nutty, puttee, putty, rutty, smutty.

-uture, future, moocher, suture.

-utler, butler, cutler, scuttler, subtler.

-uty. See **-ooty.**

-uxion. See **-uction.**

-uyer. See **-ier.**

-uzzle, guzzle, muzzle, nuzzle, puzzle.

-uzzler, guzzler, muzzler, nuzzler, puzzler.

-uzzy, fuzzy, hussy; fuzzy-wuzzy.

-yan. See **-ion.**

-yer. See **-ier.**

-ylla. See **-illa.**

-ylon, nylon, pylon, trylon.

-yly. See **-ily.**

-ymbal. See **-imble.**

-ymbol. See **-imble.**

-ymic. See **-imic.**

-yming. See **-iming.**

-yncher. See **-incher.**

-yness. See **-inus.**

-ynic. See **-inic.**

-ypsy, gypsy, ipse, tipsy; Poughkeepsie.

-yptic, cryptic, diptych, glyptic, styptic, triptych; ecliptic, elliptic; apocalyptic.

-yra. See **-ira.**

-yrant. See **-irant.**

-yrate, gyrate, irate, lyrate; circumgyrate, dextrogyrate.

-yric, lyric, Pyrrhic; butyric, empiric, satiric, satyric; panegyric.

-yron. See -iren.

-yrtle. See -urtle.

-yrus. See -irus.

-ysian. See -ision.

-ysic, phthisic, physic; metaphysic.

-ysmal. See -ismal.

-yssal. See -istle.

-ystic. See -istic.

-ytic. See -itic.

A Glossary of
Poetic Terms

accent, the stress or emphasis placed on certain syllables, usually indicated by a mark (´) above the stressed syllable. An unaccented syllable is usually indicated by a "short" mark (˘) above the syllable. Example:

Had we but world enough, and time

alexandrine, a line of verse consisting of six iambic feet. Example:

All clad | in Lin|coln green, | with caps | of

red | and blue |

alliteration, the repetition of the same consonant sound or sound group, especially in initial stressed syllables. Example:

The *s*oft *s*weet *s*ound of *S*ylvia'*s* voice

amphibrach, a foot consisting of an unaccented syllable followed by an accented and an unaccented syllable. Example (the first three feet are amphibrachs):

The clans are | impatient | and chide thy | delay |

amphimacer, a foot consisting of an accented syllable followed by an unaccented syllable and an accented syllable. Example:

Catch a star, | falling fast |

anapest, a foot consisting of two unaccented syllables followed by one accented syllable. Example:

Never hear | the sweet mu|sic of speech |

assonance, the use of identical vowel sounds in several words, often as a substitute for rhyme. Example:

Shr*i*nk h*i*s th*i*n essence like a r*i*veled flow'r

ballad, 1. a simple narrative poem of popular origin, composed in short stanzas, often of a romantic nature and adapted for singing. **2.** any poem written in such a style.

ballade, a poem consisting (usually) of three stanzas having an identical rhyme scheme, followed by an envoy. The final line of each stanza and the envoy is the same.

ballad stanza, a four-line stanza in which the first and third lines are in iambic tetrameter while the second and fourth lines are in iambic trimeter; the second and fourth lines rhyme. In a common variant, the alternate lines rhyme. Example:

> They followed from the snowy bank
>   Those footsteps one by one,
> Into the middle of the plank—
>   And further there was none.

blank verse, unrhymed verse in iambic pentameter, usually not in formal stanza units.

caesura, the main pause in a line of verse, usually near the middle. Example:

Know then thyself, || presume not God to scan

cinquain, a stanza consisting of five lines.

consonance, the use of an identical pattern of consonants in different words. Examples:

time—tome—team—tame
fall—fell—fill—full
slow—slew—slay—sly

closed couplet, a couplet whose sense is completed within its two lines. Example:

True wit is nature to advantage dress'd,
What oft was thought, but ne'er so well
express'd.

couplet, two consecutive lines that rhyme. Example:

Touch her not scornfully;
Think of her mournfully.

dactyl, a foot consisting of one accented syllable followed by two unaccented syllables. Example:

Cannon to | right of them |

dimeter, a line of verse consisting of two feet.

distich, a couplet

elegy, a subjective, meditative poem, especially one that expresses grief or sorrow.

envoy, 1. a short stanza concluding a poem in certain archaic metrical forms. **2.** a postscript to a poetical composition, sometimes serving as a dedication.

epic, a long narrative poem about persons of heroic stature and actions of great significance, and conforming to a rigid organization and form.

epigram, a short and pithy remark, often in verse.

feminine ending, an ending on a word in which the final syllable is unaccented. Examples:

> softness, careful, another, fairest

foot, the metrical unit in poetry, consisting of one accented syllable and one or more unaccented syllables. The most commonly found feet are iamb, anapest, dactyl, and trochee. The foot is usually marked in scansion by a vertical line. Example:

> I am mon|arch of all | I survey |

free verse, verse that does not adhere to a fixed pattern of meter, rhyme, or other poetic conventions.

heptameter, a line of verse consisting of seven feet.

heroic couplet, two consecutive rhyming lines in iambic pentameter. Example:

> O thoughtless mortals! ever blind to fate,
> Too soon dejected, and too soon elate.

hexameter, a line of verse consisting of six feet.

iamb, a foot consisting of one unaccented syllable followed by one accented syllable. Example:

The cúr|few tólls | the knéll | of párt|ing

day |

internal rhyme, a rhyme that occurs within a
line. Example:

> So *slight* the *light*
> I could not see,
> My *fair*, dear *Clair*,
> That it was thee.

Italian sonnet, a sonnet written in iambic
pentameter with a rhyme scheme of *abba
abba cde dde*. There are occasional variants
of the rhyme scheme in the last six lines.
The first eight lines (the *octave*) usually
present a theme or premise; the last six lines
(the *sestet*) present the conclusion or resolution.

limerick, a five-line poem using trimeters for
the first, second, and fifth lines and using
dimeters for the third and fourth lines. It is
usually written in a mixture of amphibrachs
and iambs.

lyric, a poem with a particularly musical,
songlike quality.

macaronic verse, verse in which two or more
languages are interlaced.

masculine ending, an ending on a word in
which the final syllable is accented. Examples:

resound, avoid, reply, consume

meter, the basic rhythmic description of a line
in terms of its accented and unaccented

syllables. Meter describes the sequence and relationship of all the syllables of a line.

monometer, a line of verse consisting of one foot.

nonometer, a line of verse consisting of nine feet.

octave, the first eight lines of an Italian sonnet.

octometer, a line of verse consisting of eight feet.

ode, a poem, usually complicated in its metrical and stanzaic form, on a highly serious or particularly important theme.

onomatopoeia, the quality of a word that imitates the sound it designates. Examples:

> honk, bang, tintinnabulation

ottava rima, a stanza written in iambic pentameter with a rhyme scheme of *ababcc*.

pastoral, a poem dealing with simple rural life.

pentameter, a line of verse consisting of five feet.

Petrarchan sonnet. See **Italian sonnet.**

quatrain, a stanza consisting of four lines.

refrain, an expression, a line, or a group of lines that is repeated at certain points in a poem, usually at the end of a stanza.

rhyme, an identity of certain sounds in different words, usually the last words in two or more lines.

rhyme royal, a stanza written in iambic pentameter with a rhyme scheme of *ababbcc*.

rhyme scheme, the pattern of rhyme used in a stanza or poem.

rondeau, a poem consisting of three stanzas of five, three, and five lines, using only two rhymes throughout. A refrain appears at the end of the second and third stanzas.

rondel, a poem consisting (usually) of fourteen lines on two rhymes, of which four are made up of the initial couplet repeated in the middle and at the end (the second line of the couplet sometimes being omitted at the end).

rondelet, a poem consisting of five lines on two rhymes, the opening word or words being used after the second and fifth lines as an unrhymed refrain.

run-on line, a line which does not end at a point of sense at which there would normally be a pause in speech.

scansion, the process of indicating the pattern of accented and unaccented syllables in a line of verse.

septet, a stanza consisting of seven lines.

sestet, a group of six lines, especially those at the end of a sonnet.

sestina, a poem of six six-line stanzas and a three-line envoy, originally without rhyme, in which each stanza repeats the end words of the lines of the first stanza, but in different order. The envoy uses these six end words again, three in the middle of the lines and three at the end.

Shakespearian sonnet, a sonnet written in iambic pentameter with a rhyme scheme of *abab cdcd efef gg*. The theme is often presented in the three quatrains and the poem is concluded with the couplet.

sight rhyme, not a rhyme but two or more

words which end in identical spelling.
Examples:

> though, bough, through

slant rhyme, an approximate rhyme, usually
characterized by assonance or consonance.

song, a short and simple poem, usually suitable
for setting to music.

sonnet, a poem consisting of fourteen lines in
iambic pentameter. The most common forms
are the Italian sonnet (which see) and the
Shakespearian sonnet (which see).

Spenserian stanza, a stanza consisting of eight
iambic pentameter lines and a final iambic
hexameter line, with a rhyme scheme of
ababbcbcc.

spondee, a foot consisting of two accented
syllables. Example:

> Speak soft, | stand still |

stanza, a fixed pattern of lines or rhymes, or
both.

stress. See **accent.**

tercet, a group of three consecutive lines that
rhyme together or relate to an adjacent
tercet by rhymes.

terza rima, a poem in iambic meter consisting
of eleven-syllable lines arranged in tercets,
the middle line of each tercet rhyming with
the first and third lines of the following
tercet.

tetrameter, a line of verse consisting of four
feet.

trimeter, a line of verse consisting of three feet.

triolet, an eight-line stanza in which line 1 recurs as line 4 and line 7, while line 2 recurs as line 8.

triplet, a stanza consisting of three lines.

trochee, a foot consisting of one accented syllable followed by one unaccented syllable. Example:

Why so | pale and | wan, fond | lover |

vers de société, a light-spirited and witty poem, usually brief, dealing with some social fashion or foible.

verse, 1. one line of a poem. **2.** a group of lines in a poem. **3.** any form in which rhythm is regularized.

villanelle, a poem consisting of (usually) five tercets and a final quatrain, using only two rhymes throughout.

weak rhyme, rhyme which falls upon the unaccented (or lightly accented) syllables.